KINGS and PROPHETS, PRESIDENTS and POLITICS

KINGS and PROPHETS, PRESIDENTS and POLITICS

Donald Jarboe

LIBERTY HILL PRESS

Liberty Hill Press
2301 Lucien Way #415
Maitland, FL 32751
407.339.4217
www.libertyhillpublishing.com

Table Of Contents

1

Introduction

T he election of Donald Trump in 2016 changed everything. Trump's desire was to "Make America Great Again"- which was the slogan of his campaign. Obama failed to deliver on his campaign slogan of "Hope" and "Change we can believe in" rather after eight years of what was known as the Great Recession instead our American economy was on deaths' door, even in spite of billions of dollars of Obama's "stimulus money" Obama was unable to alleviate the nation's suffering.

The economy would however make a dramatic turnaround in the anticipation of the coming newly elected President. Even before Trump's Inauguration, the stock market was experiencing record up turns. Trump believed, as did many, that the once great America had been on the decline and without some kind of "divine intervention" we were hopelessly falling on a downward death spiral. Soon, the once great America, would cease to exist.

Only to the astute observer, the informed citizen, and those of us who had not yet been "brainwashed" we seemed to know we were only, possibly, a few more years of ungodly liberal leadership, away from disaster, that is, the end of what we know today as the great United States of America.

Trump recognized this decline, as did many, and this was what he saw as his duty and obligation to bring about change. As a show of sincerity, Trump has also committed and continues to donate, his entire government salary to charity. How many liberals do you know that are willing to do this?

People need to wake up and see it is God who put this man in office for the good of the people. Yet, many of these same people ignorantly, arrogantly, and fervently oppose him at every turn. Sadly, many of these same persons would happily roll out the red carpet for the antichrist. Unfortunately, this includes Pastors and many Christians who refuse to use the scriptures to determine their vote.

Trump, as a person who benefited and prospered greatly, thanks to the freedom and opportunity affording to him by the great United States, he understood that it was not socialism, nor communism, that made America great. But rather, one nation under God, with its free markets, capitalism, equal opportunity for all- all made possible by a government for the people and by the people. Including a moral acknowledgement and understanding of the Judeo-Christian God of the Bible.

This book will present a Biblical case for understanding our current political crisis in America. I believe the LORD impressed on me that there is coming a change to our "usual" political environment. Certainly, recent wide-spread protests and liberal calls for nation-wide mail-in voting are some new aspects. We may have to watch and see how things go, but for now, I believe as never before, that America is in a crucial time both morally, culturally, and what should be quite obvious to everyone, "politically."

I believe the overall future of America literally hangs in the balance. While at the same time, the overall future of "global elitists ambitions" and their desire for a "one world government" hangs in the balance as well. The results of this up and coming Presidential election will chart the course for the American people for many years to come. Also, the political challenges we may face in 2024 and beyond may be difficult to predict at this time.

So why is this election cycle so different than those that came before? It is because we are in a time like no other in our history. Not only are we teetering on the brink of global change as never before, these times are unparalleled in the modern history or recent memory. The ancient scriptures are being fulfilled at an alarming rate. We are living in the days as significant as the days when Christ walked the earth. Could it be that our world is on the apex of one world or GLOBAL Government?

Well, plans implemented long ago, which have continued throughout generations and throughout times past, have all carefully, methodically, and maliciously brought us to an apex of the global elites' sinister plans. They desire to bring the nations of the world under one centralized power base from which they can dictate complete control over the masses. For the "global elites", there are however two main problems right now that are "stifling" or delaying their fulfillment of their much anticipated and "sinister plans". They are predominately President Trump and the good people of the United States of America.

Truly, right now, global ambitions could be realized sooner rather than later with the right catalyst. In other words, the recent and even current Covid-19 pandemic should be showing us a possible glimpse into some future, yet to be realized, "up and coming" global event. That would easily change everything we know about what we think about our future. So, take note, this virus occurred on a global scale, I believe this is unique, prophetically. It may be perhaps a cloaked or "veiled" glimpse of some coming future scenario that warrants some kind of global united response or solution. Again, we may have to wait and see!

For right now, I believe God is wanting to get our attention. I, for one, want to listen. The words of the prophets of old, faithfully foretold in scripture, are now converging in conjunction with the global elites' aspirations unlike any other time previously. This book will uncover some of those hidden prophetic and profound truths found in scripture. This book is meant to be a "wake-up call" to all those who can receive it.

So, where are we, prophetically? Well I believe we have some time! I also believe we have no time to waste. We should all allow time in our busy lives to gradually but faithfully "get our house in order". Many of us need to become familiar with end-time scripture including the book of Revelation and Mathew chapter 24, -it might be wise to take this time to prepare for hard times in the future. We do not want to forget the lessons from Covid-19. Remember the empty shelves at the grocery store and the selling out of some critical supplies.

It is also time that we consider whether we are in right-standing with God (or not), make any necessary changes, then continue to encourage our friends, family and loved ones to do the same. It takes time to learn the truth and be able to live by faith. For Christians, it takes time to grow and mature into "strong believers", it does not necessarily happen over-night. I will guarantee that coming events in our future will most assuredly require a mature, faith-filled Christian response.

So, will you heed the call or will you be caught off-guard when Biblical events unfold in an unprecedented level around you? It is time that we all faithfully stand in the gap; with prayers and petitions to God until such time that we see our friends, family, and loved ones, come into the knowledge of the truth. It is so easy to go on through life as if nothing will happen or nothing has changed, and yet we must "resist" the temptation to do so.

We all must realize the significance of our day. The fact is, the fulfillment of a world government has not been attempted on this level since the Ancient Tower of Babel, see (Genesis 11:1-9)

Genesis 11:1 "...and the whole earth was of one language, and of one speech."

While mankind (as a whole) joined forces to build this great tower, God however, was not pleased. There He confounded their speech, so the people were dispersed across the globe according to their ability to share a common language. The building of the tower was an act of defiance against God. Today's global aspirations are no different.

To some, even many, the idea appears to be a good one. To the secular (without God) understanding, it may appear benevolent, maybe a good solution to some of the world's ills, even a time when the limits on mankind's human ability might reach some historical, unprecedented leap in collective consciousness. A great many will wholeheartedly believe this lie, particularly at first. However, instead it will culminate into the worst, disastrous time in all history known as the great tribulation, Math 24:21 says: "**For then shall be great tribulation, such as was not since the beginning of the world to this time, no, nor ever shall be.**"

You see, when we have a good look at the truth of the Bible, we can free ourselves from the lies and deception so prevalent in our society by learning, believing, and understanding God's Word. Because of the fall of man in the Garden of Eden, see Genesis chapter 3, we have an inherent issue of our sinful nature, therefore, apart from God we will not be successful at reaching some great spiritual plateau, some great awakening, or some transformative new age.

Unfortunately, a great many people will fall for this lie, for the Devil is a liar, John 8:44: "**...for he is a liar, and the father of it.**" And it says he will deceive the whole world, Rev 12:9: "**...that old serpent, called the Devil, and Satan, which deceiveth the whole world...**" Even now there are so many already deceived and unless they have a life changing encounter with the Lord Jesus Christ, they may be lost forever.

In Matthew chapter 4:8: there is an intriguing account between Jesus and the Devil which plays out over who is the rightful heir involving the world's kingdoms and governments.

"**The devil taketh Him (Jesus) up into an exceeding high mountain and sheweth Him all the kingdom's of the world, and the glory of them; and saith unto Him, all these things will I give thee if thou wilt fall down and worship me. Then saith Jesus** unto Him, get thee hence Satan, for it is written, thou shalt worship the Lord thy God, and Him only shalt thou serve."

This was a genuine temptation to Jesus because he is the rightful coming world leader- one day He will sit on the throne of His own government here on Earth. Isaiah 9:6: "**...and the government shall be upon his shoulder...**"

Jesus will be coming back to deal with the Devil and those people who choose to follow him. Yet, we know through scripture, prior to that day, Satan will attempt to control the world in his effort to replace God, similarly to the recent attempt of Adolf Hitler's desire to rule the world. Yet, this time it will be like no other time in history, that is what the Word says. Hitler's attempt was only temporarily successful and on a much smaller scale. The Bible hints that the coming antichrist world dictator will on some level affect the entire world. Rev 3:10: "**... hour of temptation, which shall come upon all the world...**"

Most students of Biblical prophecy all conclude we are now living in times like no other. I will try to emphasize throughout this book just how powerful the prophetic scriptures can be. For example, the book of Revelation is becoming more relevant today than at any other time previously. Prophecy, and its fulfillment, is also used in scripture as evidence of its divine nature with the Almighty. With each additional verse of scripture, the case for the truth just keeps building and strengthening even more and more.

How few have even realized that the nations and leaders of the world, have been quietly choosing sides building and dismantling alliances and testing each other's resolve. Some openly, sometimes secretly, yet all <u>intuitively,</u> are the nations of the world sensing some yet unknown future global show-down such as foretold in Revelation Chapter 6.

In fact, war or threat of war may be the necessary catalyst to justify and initiate world government on a large scale. Just as the United States are politically, even culturally, divided down the center, so too is the world divided across the same or similar lines as well.

The need, or perceived need, is there for some united global response to such issues as the current pandemic, climate change, overpopulation, less-stable nations' aspirations for nuclear weapons, potential and real widespread droughts and famines, the continuing illegal drug trade (which further ignites gang violence) crime across borders, the slow, methodical push for a global currency, the sex trade and human trafficking and so much more. These needs are being magnified now more than ever.

So, what is wrong with a global response to the world's problems or a one world government? Well, there is nothing wrong with a global government per se. For one day, all the world will be under one leadership and prosperous, and yet, this is not the time for that world government. Because before we get there, God is going to allow man to govern the world without Him. All the world will see and live with the result of man's global governance, under Satan and without God.

Believe me, it is NOT going to be good and I certainly do not want to be around without God's sovereign protection. It will be a global nightmare with the deception that it is the answer to the world's problems. It will likely begin so benevolent that many, at first, will be onboard. Many will sing it's praises however it will prove to be the worst time in recorded history- a time of unparalleled evil and utter destruction as never before. God will pour out His wrath on those who "believed not" on His only begotten Son, JESUS CHRIST, the Savior of the world. Acts 4:12: **"For there is none other name under heaven given among men, whereby we must be saved."** Amen- I just had to preach the truth there!!!

So, this book will uncover centuries old, written verses, within the pages of the Bible that contain incredible and very accurate predictions or prophecies about the "state of our union" that we can quite easily observe in today's American political landscape. This book will hopefully show you a small example of just how powerful the Word of God can be and how vital it is to know and understand the scriptures for our own lives. In fact, we all need to become scholars in our own right, by studying the Bible for ourselves. No one can do that for us, yet there are plenty of helpful resources available.

God wants to reveal Himself through the teaching of the scriptures to each one of us who come to Him for hope, guidance, direction, and truth. We are blessed in this nation to be able to go to a local bookstore, or even stores such as Walmart, to pick up a copy of God's Word for ourselves. We have also been provided such vast resources of different Bible versions, parallel Bibles, study aids such as concordances, commentaries, and Bible dictionaries, as well as books written on nearly every aspect of God's Word and man's interaction with Him.

So many rich resources are available to us in the country, yet many do not take advantage of these liberties so richly afforded to us. In many parts of the world, this just simply is not the case. However, so tragically, many Americans are completely illiterate of God's written Word. They often go about spouting their beliefs however, the Bible clearly states in Matthew 4:4: **"Man shall not live on bread alone, but by every word that proceeds out of the mouth of God."** Even as our daily bread is vital for life, our "spiritual food" is equally as vital according to God. Bible illiteracy may be the most serious issue facing our younger generations in this country.

The freedoms and prosperity Americans enjoy today are a direct result of adhering to the guiding principles founded in scripture. The millions of believers and faithful followers of Jesus Christ in this nation- including our own founding fathers- sought out the freedoms and liberties to preserve the right to worship and serve God as they see fit, without government restrictions or intrusions of any kind. There has certainly been much blood shed to earn, preserve, and protect these very rights. Unfortunately, these principles are under attack today in our country and quietly have been for decades now.

The liberal leaders and politicians in our nation today seek to silence the Christian majority, simply ignoring our Christian heritage altogether, either by ignorance or purposeful actions. They deliberately seek and methodically act to remove or erase every conservative Christian value and representation from the political and social landscape. They have very successfully progressed at attempting to silence every voice, every believer, as well as every historical use of scripture and Christian symbolism, to include the removal of public displays of the Ten Commandments, and do not forget the (Obama-era) attacks on public displays of our Christmas time "nativity scenes" and other reminders of our Christian heritage.

Basically, to kick God out of government, schools, media, and so on. It is like shooting yourself in the foot. It is not going to turn out well for these people, nor for the nation and governments that they undermine. They seek to change our long held traditional beliefs. Do not be a part of this for, again, it will not work out well for you. Are you stronger than God? Are you going to counsel GOD ALMIGHTY? That is a bad idea. If this describes you, please, come to your senses. Acts 3:19 says: **"Repent ye therefore and be converted that your sins may be blotted out."**

<u>I am laying out a Biblical case and basis for the people of this great nation to come back to God for some, and to come to God for the first time for others</u>. This would be the best thing that you could do for yourself, your future, your family and for your country. I base that on the scriptures and my firsthand experience

with God for over 25 years. I do not base that on my own human reasoning, thoughts, or intelligence. Sadly, many "base" their beliefs on everything under the sun, and without any reliable, legitimate, or confirmable source. God did not leave us helpless, that is why He left us the Word of God.

Do not let yourselves or another's opinion influence you into believing that the HOLY BIBLE is anything less than <u>God's exclusive source for truth</u> in this world. There is not another book like it in all the world! It can change your life. As I said before, Jesus Christ can prove Himself to anybody who is willing to sincerely seek Him. You can have an amazing experience with the one true GOD for yourself, and I pray many will do so.

I also pray for the believers who would dare to vote contrary to the truth found in scripture. We are living in a time where we must be accountable for our actions. It is our duty to know the truth in any given situation and to act on that revealed truth. We are told in Joshua 1:8: **"Let not this book of the law depart from thine eyes, but mediate on it day and night that thou may observe to do according to all that is written therein."** This principle is echoed throughout scripture- it is time for the Church to stand together as a force for good in the world.

For far too long, the Church has fallen silent in the face of evil. When they took Bibles out of the school, the Church did nothing. When they replaced Creationism with Evolution, we failed to change it. When they legalized all forms of abortion, the Church remained silent. Same sex marriage, nothing. And now, there are forces in America that want to destroy everything this nation represents for good. We must learn from the mistakes of the past.

I believe the Church today is much more lethal to the enemy than it once was, our republic is fragile and must be upheld by the actions of good men and good women. Many in this world would desire to see America's influence to the rest of the world, falter, leaving all manner of evil dictators, free reign and without restraint or accountability. Do not get me wrong, I know America is not perfect. We have made our share of mistakes, but much of the world should be thankful to America in many ways. Because of our Godly heritage, the United States has helped many across the globe in countless ways- including spreading the gospel. Surely, we have stood in the way against many great evils in this world. This can only be done with a strong America.

I am pleading with Christians that either do not vote or that vote contrary to scripture. For many, it may not be wise to vote according to how your mom and dad voted or vote, neither by political parties that make claims to your allegiance (based on race or economic classes) or whatever party will do this or that. It is time for all of that to change. It is time that we honor GOD at the ballot box in November- DO NOT SIT OUT THIS ELECTION! Uphold and stand for the truth. It is more important today than perhaps any other time in history. There is a lot at stake!

Our world is being shaken. America is on the verge of becoming unrecognizable as the place many grew up and remember. We are not there yet, however, there are forces at work- some hidden and others at the forefront- whose desire is to reinvent America to align with the minds of wealthy and powerful elites. The ruthless, anti-Christian, self-serving, and ungodly persons seek a world far different than the vision our founding fathers once had. They gave everything and pledged forth their lives, liberty, and property to establish this great republic. America has strayed far from our Christian Judeo values that many still hold dear.

Today is a call to arms for prayer for this great nation to stand and to join with our many Christian intercessors and prayer warriors. We are in a fight for the soul of America and I am calling on Americans everywhere to take a stand this November 3rd, 2020 Presidential election and future elections as well. It is our duty to uphold our precious American values and freedoms that we have long enjoyed. People must renew their minds. So many have not comprehended the shift taking place here in America and across the globe. This nation has been blessed! We have enjoyed the benefits of peace and prosperity for so long in this country that we totally take it for granted.

It is just so easy to simply sit down in front of the TV and think things are as they always were, and things will be as they've always been. This is so deceptive and pervasive, and it is so tempting to sit on the couch while preoccupied with worldly pursuits. You know, the cares of this life, the day to day routine, etc. As a result, so many may totally miss it. WE MUST OPEN OUR EYES!! I want to emphasize the fact that nothing could be further from the truth. I want to set forth in this book a look or glimpse of what is really going on and what to do about it. This book contains scriptural truth that will unveil liberal lies far more than a simple voters' guide could do.

I will make the Biblical case for today's political environment and hopefully cause many to see and understand for themselves, become informed citizens. We must free ourselves from the deadly influence of lies, deceptions, and propaganda purveying this society. We will compare your belief systems to that of the Bible and "think and act" in agreement with GOD ALMIGHTY and none other. Because if you do not get a heavy dose of truth today and act upon it, tomorrow could be too late.

Sadly, some will just be sitting there when the lights go off, draw back the curtain, have a look outside, and behold a different world, thinking "How did I get here? What just happened?" They will be left totally unprepared, completely caught off guard, and thinking this must be some kind of bad dream- with lots of questions and too few answers- completely vulnerable and subject to some new reality which is out of their control, and left wondering what is next.

But FEAR NOT- there is another scenario which is far better, so please read on. Get this information into your mind, open your heart, be teachable, be objective, give this book a chance, and get your mind renewed. There is plenty of truth and plenty of scriptures to support the ideas presented here. Then, last of all, please share this book with a loved one. Be blessed and I pray that God will open your understanding.

In fact, King Solomon, <u>the King that had everything</u> and authored the book of Ecclesiastes, came to the realization that worldly pursuits and efforts apart from God are all vanity. The Hebrew word for vanity can mean "to lead astray." He ends his writings saying in Ecclesiastes 12:13: **"Let us hear the conclusion of the whole matter: Fear GOD and keep His commandments: for this is the whole duty of man."**

This really tells it like it is and sums it up. If we really understood scripturally what life was all about, we would not hesitate to pursue the things of God. We would freely give God His rightful place in our lives, which includes KNOWING HIS WORD (The Bible) and how it applies to the situations and circumstances of everyday life. We could judge matters based on the truth revealed in His written Word which may have eternal rewards, both now and in the future. So, thanks for reading this and get ready to be blown away!

Hebrews 10:7: ...''believing all things which are written in the law and the prophets.''

2

Basis Of All Truth

The Seventy

The story goes, King Ptolemy of Egypt, with the blessing of the high priest and Sanhedrin in Jerusalem, took on the task of presiding over the translation of the Hebrew Torah. This new translation would be the first Greek language version of its kind. The name of the new translation would come to be known as the "Septuagint" or Latin for "seventy." It got its name from the King's protocol to assemble seventy, some say seventy-two, translators. Each were placed in separate rooms and, once separated, all were told to translate the same portion of the Hebrew text.

Once completed, the seventy translations were compared, it was found that each translation of the seventy were identical. Obviously, those involved could not help but to acknowledge the miraculous event described as an "open miracle"- just an example of the "hand of God" guiding and directing and fulfilling His will and purpose for His written Word.

The Bible Codes

Another interesting subject relating to the supernatural origins of scripture would be the "Bible Codes"- what some call the Torah codes. The Bible Codes are simply the use of numerical patterns applied to portions of scripture. The combining letters, once assembled, reveal intelligent groups of words, including numbers which may produce relevant dates as well.

The idea is nothing new, in fact, and has been thought about for centuries on a small scale. One example would be the story of Isaac Newton, a well-known 17th century scientist and theologian. Legend goes that Newton was hit on the head with a falling apple while sitting beneath the tree and this somehow sparked his genius, causing him to develop his famous theory on the law of gravity. This same Newton also believed in some manner of coded revelation hidden within the scriptures, although he was not able to prove his theory before his death. He certainly had prophetic insight into the divine attributes of the Word of God.

Really, it was not until the access to modern computer technology, fulfilling God's plan and timing, that the theory, practice, and outcome became well known and significant. Researchers were developing astonishing results, popularized by many books on the subject around the late 90's. One such popular book on the subject would be the "Bible Code" by Michael Drosnin, published in 1997.

These random numeric sequences or codes, called "equidistant letter sequencing"- when applied to scripture, were producing intelligent word groupings describing well known actual historical events. For example, relevant word groupings located in brief collections of verses in the book of Deuteronomy produced such detailed word groupings far beyond the laws of probability or random chance.

One group, named the "Holocaust" coding's discovered numerous descriptive words contained within the same portion of scripture, as follows: Hitler, Mein Kampf, Fuehrer, Germany, Holocaust, Genocide, Auschwitz, Crematorium, and more.

Other non-historical groupings were discovered as well. A chapter in the book of Genesis, relating to the story of the creation, found numerous recognizable common names for trees, animals, and the Creator's name, "Yeshua"- hidden and encoded in the text. The name of Jesus, His disciples, and descriptions of His life, ministry, and gospels were found encoded between two chapters of Isaiah. These are but a few examples and the lists go on...

Because this revelation is so damaging to the kingdom of darkness, numerous critics, liberal Christians included, have attempted to discredit legitimate bible code research and findings. Some less credible researchers have attempted to use these techniques to try and predict the future. I do not believe this is God's intention. Those who attempt to predict the future through Bible codes are in murky waters. These Bible codes simply point to a supreme intelligent creator and divine authority.

These same numerical code techniques have been tested on several significant secular and religious books and writings as well, including the Muslim proclaimed, "holy book", the Koran. No book apart from the Bible has ever produced equal results, or even come close to the phenomenon produced when adhering to the same standard of protocols.

Truly the Bible is a supernatural book that stands alone in the vast confusion of texts and teachings that abound. From self-proclaimed prophets and religious leaders, to philosophies and sciences that attempt to lay hold on the exclusive right held by the Bible alone as the ONE reliable, truthful, and divinely inspired revelation to all mankind. The one and only Bible!

If you would like to further learn about the Bible codes, just beware that there is a quite literal "snake pit" of confusing literature and opinions on the topic. Do not allow skeptics and unbelievers to take away from the beauty and great work that God has done, for I barely scratched the surface on this topic.

Few people realize that we used to pray and read Bible verses in our public schools in this country. In fact, the Board of Education used to supply copies of the King James Bible to our schools that is so powerful! There was a time when Bibles were used as textbooks in our schools. How many of us realize that many of our colleges and universities were founded by Christians in this country? I am talking about, Yale, Harvard, Princeton, and many others. Harvard, our oldest university, was named after the "Reverend" John Harvard.

The original document known as the "Rules and Precepts of Harvard" reads in part, as follows, *"Let every student be plainly instructed, and earnestly pressed to consider well, the main end of his life and studies, to know God and Jesus Christ which is eternal life, John 17:3, and therefore to lay Christ in the bottom, as the only foundation of all sound knowledge and learning. And seeing the Lord only giveth wisdom..."* Does that sound like a secular university to you? I tell you, these institutions need to come "back" to God, and not the other way around! It would be good to read the entire document, which continues to reference the scripture and Christian values throughout.

The Bible is so relevant and important today, it is more precious than gold. Without it, mankind would believe just about anything, this is especially true "today" in these difficult times. Let me tell you, what a man believes can be powerful! What you believe can send you to heaven or can send you to hell. A very frightening reality. Your beliefs might cause you to strap a bomb across your back or it might cause you to fly a jet plane, full of people, into a tall building.

Again, what we believe can be powerful. That is why we sometimes need to, take a step back and carefully consider what exactly it is that we do in fact believe! When I first believed in Jesus Christ, God confirmed to me that he Himself was indeed very real according to scripture. These included answers to prayers, and many other practical ways, and He continues to do so every day since then. Whatever you believe, I urge you to take it to God, open your Bible and if you don't have one- what are you waiting for? It is still the bestselling book of all time. God Almighty didn't leave us in the dark but provided us with a great resource for truth. That's why we will be held accountable and we are without excuse!

Some may recall from their history lessons, a time in European history commonly known as the "dark ages" these began in the fifth century after the fall of Rome, in the year 476, and lasted for about one-thousand years. I believe these dark ages were a direct result of the absence of Biblical truth for the common man! This absence of truth would allow unsavory individuals to take advantage of the masses, as did the early Roman Catholic Church. It was a time when the Church developed their own unbiblical doctrines and beliefs. This was also a time when the hierarchy of the Church went about brutally silencing all decenters and con- tradictory versions of their "universal beliefs."

They taught that the "Roman Catholic Church" was supreme, and the Pope himself was "infallible" a term used exclusively for God alone. They taught that the Bible and its interpretations were not suitable for the "unlearned or common people" rather they would only be left to interpretation by their own clergy!

The people, without the Bible as a measuring rod or stan- dard of truth and error, hopelessly fell victim to the cruel and unusual demands of the so-called church. With their sometimes outlandish, shocking, and heretical teachings and beliefs. One such teaching was called "indulgences" this is where people were told to give money to the church in exchange for the forgiveness of sins and to ensure their entrance into heaven. How convenient for the church and their clergy members.

Many believed this lie and without access to the scriptures themselves how could they dispute these "doctrines." Many of these same doctrines and beliefs are still in existence today. These include such beliefs as purgatory, relics, the rosary and many more. These are beyond the scope and teaching for this book, however there are many great resources on the subject.

These Dark Ages seem to come to a climax around the time of the "Bubonic plague or Black Plague" that is, from the years, 1346 to 1353, This just happened to be the worst plague in recorded history. Approximately a third of Europeans died from this plague. Covid-19 doesn't even come close! It was at this time when the common people began to question the power and authority of the Pope and of the Roman Catholic Church. It was because they seemed incapable of promoting ant kind of relief or aid in this disastrous moment. Surely, they must have been preoccupied. It was not until, finally, the Protestant Reformation of 1517 which would bring the needed change and relief for the Christian believers.

Next, to set the stage for the Protestant Reformation, something very important, had to happen first! That was in the year 1455, when, Johann Gutenberg (inventor of the moveable-type printing press) completed the first Bible ever in printed form. The Gutenberg Bible, of which some copies still exist to this day. It would be the first complete Bible that was not painstakingly compared and copied by hand.

This certainly paved the way for a complete compilation of the scriptures to be made available for the common man, this was of course God's intention all the time. Now, mankind would finally have access to the available resources to confidently "test the spirits" and to judge and discern right from wrong for themselves. Prior to this time, complete copies of the scripture, where rare and expensive, and out of reach of the common people.

I have included the following account of the Biblical story of the prophet Elijah and his dealings with the popular, government sanctioned "false prophets" of his day. Elijah presented the people with a simple but powerful argument, and one that is still relevant, especially today! That is simply this, If God is GOD! Then follow him! Or if <u>Baal</u> (fill in the blank) be God then follow Baal right? That should just be common sense, right? So, where are you in this equation?

I Kings 18:21-27 (NCV) **"How long will you <u>decide between two choices</u>? If the Lord is the true God, follow Him, but if Baal is the true god, Follow Him..." "You prophets of Baal, pray to your god and I will pray to the Lord."**- verse 24: **"The God who answers... is the true God."** So, 'verse 26, **"they prayed to Baal from morning unto noon shouting "Baal, answer us!" But there was no sound, and no one answered..."** So, verse 27, **"Elijah began to make fun of them. "Pray louder" he said. "If Baal really is a God, maybe he is thinking or busy or traveling. Maybe he is sleeping so you will have to wake him!"**

As the story goes, the one true God answered by fire that day and proved Himself strong, while the false god of Baal fell silent, regardless of the prophets of Baal's passionate and persistent requests. You know there are only two choices in this life! There is the God of the Bible, then there is everything and everyone else!

I Kings 8:60: **"That all the people of the earth may know that the Lord is God and that there is none else."** What a powerful statement! If all the world knew the one true and only God, there would not be much purpose for this book. We would not have competing political parties, everyone would basically have the same general moral compass, or standard of truth. Unfortunately, that is not the case here. Our political parties could not be more divided. So, I Kings 8:60-has yet to be realized and its fulfillment will occur sometime in the future. As for now we have a great "political" divide in this country. <u>The reason for the great-divide-is one topic this book will address.</u>

However, I have learned not to base my opinions on personal feelings, or who I have been told to vote for based on tradition or across ethnic or racial lines, or even economic factors, as has been the case in the past. We can no longer afford to depend on these sources as our basis for truth, especially when it comes to our political beliefs.

We are living in a time when we must turn to the inspired Word of God, the **"Bible"** as our one and only exclusive source of truth. <u>That is perhaps the greatest reason and overall inten-tion for this book</u>. This book will reveal the true condition of our current political party's <u>great divide</u> based solely on scripture. We must understand that the Bible stands alone as the absolute final authority and written record of truth for all people, nations, and tongues- (languages).

If man would grasp this truth, literally, we would have far fewer problems in this country and society, even the world at large. I just cannot accept any argument against the fact that the Holy Bible is the unique singular revelation of God. I cannot emphasize this enough. Without God's revelation, man cannot possibly understand his purpose in this life.

However, I did not always feel this way. In fact, it was not until I had a life-changing, life-altering encounter with Jesus Christ, God the Father, and the Holy Spirit of the Bible. It was then that

I began to have my mind, beliefs, and understanding about life change (through the renewing of my mind) according to scripture.

There are so many things that are just impossible to know apart from God's revealed revelation knowledge for man. I have heard all the arguments out there against the infallibility of the Bible and they are senseless and without merit. God's Word is intended to be used in conjunction with an actual real relationship with the LORD himself. So, beware of critics that judge the Bible without the relationship to support the truths written.

Everyone must overcome their own biases concerning their beliefs of the Bible. It really does take a personal measure of faith to make the life-changing decision to stand firmly in agreement with the scriptures no matter what. God calls us to walk by faith- Romans 12:3**: "He has given to every man a measure of faith."** So, use a little faith and give the Bible the rightful place in your belief system and you will learn for yourself, as I did, the power of the written Word of God. He gave us this wonderful resource of truth for mankind's benefit and it surely has changed my life for the better- and hopefully yours as well. Because it would be impossible for a sinful, fallen man to govern himself properly apart from God, and without the knowledge contained within the scriptures. When men attempt to govern themselves apart from the Bible, they often bring a great deal of unnecessary and needless suffering to the lives of the common man- Ecclesiastes 7:20: **"For there is not a just man upon the earth that doeth good, and sinneth not."**

The halls of history are blanketed with victims of ruthless and cruel dictators. We must not allow our beloved nation to come under this unjust form of leadership. If you can accept the truths contained within this book, they should help you to have more than enough wisdom and understanding to vote in any election.

The fact is, I never once voted in any election, neither had I any interest in politics, until after my encounter with God and His teachings found within the Bible. I can still remember, thinking the common reasoning at that time that both candidates were corrupt. So, the best that I could do, would be to choose the lesser of two evils. Maybe that was true back then! However, that will not be the case of 2020 election and beyond, for there will be a clear, distinct choice- **according to scripture**.

So, I want to declare that this book will depend and rely heavily on one thing and that is the Bible. A persons' opinions, feelings, etc. just do not count here, and for good reason. If you stand with the infallibility of the Bible, you can never go wrong. You are on solid ground and you are humbly saying that your limited scope and small ability cannot compare to God's infinite wisdom. You now therefore come into proper alignment and relationship with God. That is always a good place to be!

The Bible has a wealth of information about leadership. These include records of the lives of various Kings, Princes, and authority figures and the people that they serve. Certainly, a wide range of persons and personalities throughout. The Bible gives numerous examples of both wise and good, as well as evil and tragic consequences of our daily actions. Again, there is a wealth of information contained in the scriptures, certainly too vast to cover in any single book on the subject; however, I will try to the best of my ability to present a solid case for our <u>political future</u> based on scripture and Christian-Judeo beliefs.

<u>This message to man, the Bible, is to be revered, studied, and applied to every facet of life</u>. It contains great promises, excellent benefits, and eternal hope as well for doing the same.

"Liberal" definition: "One who is open minded or not strict in the observance of **orthodox, traditional,** or **established** forms or ways."

3

Vile/Liberal

Isaiah 32:5: **"The vile person shall be no more called liberal."**
Verse 5 of Isaiah 32: is very revealing, and this is the main point! I
have numbered the text *(1-11)*-of the following verses 5-8 reads:
   **"The vile person shall be no more called liberal, *(2)* nor the
churl said to be bountiful. *(3)* For the vile person will speak vil-
lany, *(4)* and his heart will work iniquity, *(5)* to practice hypocrisy,
(6) and to utter error against the Lord, *(7)* to make empty the
soul of the hungry, and he will cause the drink of the thirsty to
fail. *(8)* The instruments also of the churl are evil: *(9)* he deviseth
wicked devices to destroy the poor with lying words, *(10)* even
when the needy speaketh right. *(11)* But the liberal deviseth
liberal things: and by liberal things shall he stand."**

Isaiah 32:5: *(1)* **"The vile person shall be no more called liberal."**

T hough written in ancient times, centuries ago, yet this verse is
   perfectly meaningful for today. This verse of scripture spells it
out, when taken in the context of our modern American political

13

debacle that is currently taking place in this country. This is a right now word and speaks to our time.

The term <u>liberal</u> is only used six times in the King James Bible, four of those times are found in the same chapter of Isaiah and used in a negative connotation. For the record, the other two are used in a positive sense. The key to this important verse of scripture is for it to be taken in the context of our modern American political landscape.

This first half of verse 5 can be so powerful! How did God know, even thousands of years ago, that the prophet Isaiah would "nail" the root cause of our political crisis? Including an accurate summary of our current "party" debacle, presently taking place in America.

How did God, in only nine words, give an exact description of today's "all too obvious" ULTRA-LIBERAL democratic political party? Here, God is saying, "you will not any longer be falsely identified as liberal as you have been" and, "you can no longer hide behind this widely accepted and benevolent term." No, God has had enough! God is wanting to remove the veil from people's eyes and help them to see the "deeper truths." Therefore, you can no longer hide under the deceptive use of the term, "liberal."

So, he has declared, in fact, I now call you vile, that is, based on your thoughts, your beliefs, and your behavior. According to the very definition of <u>vile</u> you have become *wicked, offensive, repulsive, and without standards of morality.* The Democratic Party has embraced liberal left-wing policies that no longer represent any form of decency, by God's standards. He is fed up, and he is exposing their rhetoric as vile, anti-God, and anti-Christian. This book goes into more detail, under the Chapter entitled "Issues" which covers much of the major liberal-based policies, of which, the Lord is highly opposed!

The second half of verse 5, says, *(2)* **"nor the churl said to be bountiful."** The unusual term "churl" can mean "stingy" in the Strong's Concordance so here are simply two words that are opposite from each other, just as vile and liberal should also be opposite of each other. In the next verse, vs. 6, the Lord further describes these liberals, *(3)* **"for the vile person will speak villainy."** Today, it is all over the fake-news media, they have not stopped to <u>villainize</u> this sitting President at every turn and on every issue.

Also, *(4)* **"And his heart will work iniquity"**- this poison is spewing from their "hearts"- the seat of their wicked beliefs. Their beliefs are at the core of the problem. As I have said elsewhere in this book, a person's beliefs can be powerful. It does not matter if you are sincere, you can be sincerely wrong in what you believe. God is **calling out** these vile liberals who are diametrically opposed to God's will and purpose for this great country, of which, they are wickedly destroying with their blatant disregard for Godly principles.

Verse 6: *(5)* **"To practice hypocrisy"**- the Hebrew word **"hypocrisy"** can be translated as <u>moral filth</u> again, as I've said before, just another description of the liberal political standards that they have set for themselves. (6) **"And to utter error against the Lord"**- they are not afraid to proclaim that God's ways are outdated, unenlightened, and need no longer apply to the progressive age of modern man and politics.

Verse 6 continues *(7)* **"to make empty the soul of the hungry and will cause the drink of the thirsty to fail."** Those they claim to defend, those they claim to help or stand for, well, their promises are empty, their efforts are in vain, and their solutions will not help nor bring change. Yet, God is for the "hungry" and the "thirsty" that they blindly assume allegiance to and deceptively oppress.

(8) **"The instruments also of the churl are evil."** The Google Dictionary defines "instrument" as a "tool or implement, specifically one for delicate scientific work. "a surgical instrument" Also, the term "churl" is defined as "an impolite and mean-spirited person." So, we have an interesting definition! Certainly, a surgical instrument can only describe one thing, this describes an abortion doctors "tool-kit" that is the tools of their trade. They are indeed, "evil" and no doubt these doctors have to be "mean-spirited" as well!

Verse 7 says: *(9)* **"He deviseth wicked devices to destroy the poor with lying words"**. God cares for the poor, the oppressed, and the needy. Their deceptive "wicked devises" include well thought out and wonderfully named policies and legislation. While they sound so noble indeed- yet, are filled with lies, empty promises, and deception.

So, how do they **"destroy the poor with lying words"**? Although they do this on many levels, I will tell you exactly how it is done. Let me give you one example: When you take a **poor soul** such as an already rejected, traumatized, and confused homosexual child. When you see this person who is in need of salvation (as we all are), in need of the truth set forth in scripture, in need of the power of God and genuine Christianity to intervene in their lives.

Then, instead, tell them that they are the exception that they are okay and there is nothing wrong with their identity. When you feed them lies instead of truth, when you teach them to hate Christians and hate God and tell them there is no help. When you change the laws on marriage to accommodate them. When you give them special status, when you continue to promote their lifestyle in parades, tv shows and commercials. You are doing the Devil's work! Romans 1:25; **"who changed the truth of God into a lie."**

While they deceive you into thinking all is well, yet there remains a reckoning with Almighty God, while their immortal soul may be destroyed in everlasting hell fire because they would not receive salvation. While instead of the truth, they were comforted during their brief time on the Earth. Thanks to the vile leaders who assume that if they just ignore God, perhaps His Word will not apply to them on judgment day! You see, this is a tragic tale all too common in our culture.

These liberals will one day, as will we all, need to give an account to Almighty God. Through their lies of "acceptance"- even of that which goes against nature itself (Romans 1:26)- thereby they are destroying many poor souls; and according to them there is no higher power to reckon with.

Verse 7: *(10)* "**Even when the needy speaketh right.**" Even when a person wants to do the right thing, liberals will have none of that! They will oppose you at every turn- it is their policies or no policies. For example, Trump has long hailed the proven benefits of Hydroxychloroquine. An effective drug against Covid19. It had already been approved for medical use way back in 1955. Already with strong track records by many doctors both here and abroad. Not to mention many heart-felt personal testimonies of actual Covid-19 survivors and without a whole lot of good alternatives on the market.

So, what is wrong with that! Of course, it was not their (liberals) idea, so again Trump is mercilessly villainized. Therefore, providing "life saving" medicines fall under their "propaganda protocols" therefore the common man suffers again at the expense of liberals' unjust lust for power and control- just another example of **to practice hypocrisy.**

So, the next verse says, *(11)* "**But the liberals deviseth liberal things, and by liberal things shall he stand.**" Well, it appears for the most part that the liberals are not going away. This reminds me of Daniel 12:10- **"But the wicked shall do wickedly: and none of the wicked shall understand, but the wise shall understand."** I believe, as was my case, without a genuine conversion experience with Christ, without a renewal of the mind through scripture, the liberals will keep on doing liberal things. However, It is certainly my hope that many will be converted as I have been.

The following text comes from verses 1&2- of Isaiah chapter 32, I number them *(1-4)- (1)* **"Behold, a King shall reign in righteousness,** *(2)* **and princes shall rule in judgement.** *(3)* **And a man shall be a hiding place from the wind, and a covert from the tempest;** *(4)* **as rivers of water in a dry place, as the shadow of a great rock in a weary land."**

So, now that we have covered the vile side of the argument, now I want to back up a bit to verse 1 in the very beginning of Isaiah chapter 32- *(1)* **"Behold, a King shall reign in righteousness."** Here we have contained within the same chapter as the liberal verses we just finished discussing. Take notice that this is occurring at the <u>same time</u> as those same liberal verses we discussed, as this mirrors our current political situation as well. Here we see God putting forth a King that **"shall reign in righteousness"**- (take note: this verse may also speak about the future coming of Christ, as well)

So, who else could this King describe? I am sure you know my answer, yes, Donald Trump- 45th President of the United States. Trump is God's man for this hour.

Along with Trump are *(2)* **"Princes that shall rule in judgment."** These can be described as fellow conservatives in authority, even the Judicial branch of government who make <u>judgements</u> and enforce laws based on Godly principles.

Next, verse 2 describes Trumps position of authority *(3)* **"And a man shall be as a hiding place from the wind, and a covert from the tempest."** verse 2 poetically describes Trump's win in

November 2016 and the effect it had on the good people of this nation. This verse also describes Trump as truly on the "front lines" he has been the primary target and made to endure the vicious assault and the brunt of the attack from godless liberal politicians and the fake-news media.

Finally, after eight long years of Obama, what a **relief** Trumps election was! *(4)* **"As rivers of waters in a dry place, and the shadow of a great rock in a weary land."** Well, I remember those days, and all I can say now is, thank you God, hallelujah, and Amen.

Luke 24:44, "...that all things must be fulfilled, which were written in the law of Moses, and in the prophets, and in the Psalms concerning me." (Jesus)

4

Psalms Prophecy

Introduction

Psalms chapter 1 and verse 1-says,
"Blessed is the man that walketh not in the counsel of the ungodly..."

In Part 1 of this chapter we are about to discover a prophetic unveiling of Psalms chapter 1 in the Bible. Here this psalm makes reference to the **ungodly-** this term mirrors the book of Isaiah, and his use of the term **vile.** The one thing I noticed about the ungodly is that they do not read God's Word. They do not pray. They do not seek after God. Neither is God in all their thoughts. Psalm 10:4 says: **"The wicked, through the pride of his countenance, will not seek after God."**

Many claim to be Christians and yet, neither do they take time out for daily prayer or scripture reading. They go through life thinking there are no consequences to their behavior. The ungodly would not think of kneeling to God in prayer, for themselves or on behalf of their country. Nor would they think of investigating and supporting the beliefs of our founding fathers of this Nation. By their actions they are neglecting our rich religious heritage. They are slandering the very same authors of our Constitution that these very same politicians have sworn to uphold.

The following is a quote from Abraham Lincoln: *"I have been driven many times upon my knees, by the overwhelming conviction that I had nowhere else to go. My own wisdom and that of all about me seem insufficient for that day."* This to me sounds like a man walking in humility and in right relationship with God. This is not too hard to understand. When you understand that your wisdom is "insufficient," that's when you qualify to hear the wisdom of God.

Why is it these ungodly leaders today, seem willing to give up our, and their very own rights, protections, and freedoms, regardless of the will of the people that they are called to serve. They see themselves as the rightful agents for the higher good of all. They simply totally ignore the will of "We the People" and our nation's sovereignty, to the greater ideals of an uncertain world community.

I, for one, do not want a world community led by a group of wealthy, godless, entitled, blind leaders of the blind. Matt 15:14 says: **"they are blind leaders of the blind. And if the blind lead the blind, both shall fall into the ditch."** Without Biblical wisdom, without God's thumbs up, they are destined for failure.

With Gods help, I will stand for what is right and good in this country. Not only for myself, but for our younger generations who are being bombarded daily with ungodly, vile-liberal, and socialist lies and propaganda. It is as if we have been living in some Nazi controlled German super state or even some Communist nation such as Russia, China, or other bloodthirsty, terrorists-controlled nation. What is wrong with these politicians?

Let me give something to think about. If you or your loved ones have been educated in this country after the mid- 1960s, (that is after they removed prayer and Bible reading from schools) then you missed out on an education that included faith in the God of the Bible. In fact, you may have more likely been taught political correctness (not Biblical correctness) and liberal values instead righteous ones.

Now that all started a long time ago, but it should be obvious to everyone, that over time, ultimately, our academic institutions have now finally become "corrupt." So, except for our older generations, It is probable that you or your loved ones may have succumbed to an unhealthy dose of liberal brainwashing. It is these same liberal ideals that are threatening to turn America, the greatest nation on Earth, into a weak, deprived, insignificant, and apologetic nation to the rest of the world.

Why should we apologize for being highly blessed, real life examples, of the rich faith towards the one and only true God, including a righteous government, designed by the people and for the people? Proverbs 29:2**: "When the righteous are in authority the people rejoice; when the wicked beareth rule the people mourn."** This is so true, and this is the reason why we need "righteous leadership" in this country.

In the Bible, God instructs mankind to "watch and pray." He desires His people to be aware and informed and to diligently follow Him, both in a personal relationship, and in the understanding and knowledge of the written Word- the Bible.

Many times, the Lord warns us about being caught off guard, not recognizing the signs of the times, and ignoring the things of the God. However, we can- by relationship and study of the scripture- "connect the dots" (more or less) between what the Bible teaches, foretells, and predicts, and actual events taking place around us.

It is these same events that are unfolding before our very eyes! That is, in this nation, and many other nations of the world. We are called to judge these events, in the light of scripture. We can basically search the scriptures looking for some revelation, or some actual fulfillment in our modern day.

Prophecy is simply put as a "prediction of something to come." This is not talking about divination, consulting familiar spirits, or fortune telling. These would all come under the heading of the occult, which is strictly forbidden in scripture, see (Deuteronomy chapter 18)

No, I am talking about when a man of God, a true follower of Christ, receives a communication from the Almighty, that has been captured and found written among the many authors of the 66 books of the Bible- each divinely inspired by God. II Tim 3:16 (NIV): **"All scripture is God-breathed and is useful for teaching, rebuking, correcting, and training in righteousness."**

Since God is God, He has the unique ability to predict the future. Isaiah 46:10 says: **"declaring the end from the beginning, and from ancient times the things that are not yet done, saying, my counsel shall stand, and I will do all my pleasure."** This is in fact one way that GOD ALMIGHTY confirms his deity and displays His supernatural abilities, which are far beyond man's limited capabilities. God continues to speak to His people prophetically today, however, the completed canon of scripture, the Bible, as we know it, is complete.

One final point before we get into interpreting verses in the Psalms is this: we have got to understand that we are now living in the days that the prophets foretold in scripture. There are many proofs and evidences of this. By the way, some estimate the Bible is around 25% or more prophecy, some already fulfilled, and a large majority- in my opinion- has yet to be fulfilled. It is these unfulfilled prophesies we are called to watch and pray about.

These function as signs to the believer, confirming the legitimacy of the Word, teaching us what to expect, and confirming where we are prophetically in God's timetable.

I am convinced that the generations of people alive today will experience the literal fulfillment of Bible prophecy on a scale not previously seen in modern times. Therefore, I see a literal fulfillment of Psalms Chapter 1 & 2 correlating exactly with recent and up and coming events taking place in America's political environment as we speak. NOTE- I believe we are in the <u>early</u> stages of this <u>prophetic period</u> on God's timetable, I think this "mirrors" exactly with the <u>early</u> <u>opening verses</u> in the book of Psalms. Also, these prophetic verses are setting the stage for further prophetic fulfillments in the future.

Brothers and sisters, we are living in the "days" like none other and I pray we get this. Our country is in a unique time. Never have we been more divided in this modern era than we are today. I am not talking about the days of Lincoln or the Civil War, I mean this modern era, say back to Ronald Reagan until this present day. I have never witnessed any of our Presidents endure such opposition from left-wing liberals, media institutions, and others as I have seen today.

Something has clearly changed. It is like we are in a different world. There has been a shift. I do not see the world as innocent as it once was. There are forces at work orchestrating, planning, devising, and perpetrating the downfall of America. Though this is not necessarily new, it is more in view "now" than ever before. It is no longer hiding as it once was.

What the "enemy of our souls" has been up to in this country is beginning to bear fruit and, of course, that is not in a good way. It is as if God is pulling back the curtain and we have been given the opportunity to behold the past, present, and future regarding the United States. Dark forces "working behind the scenes" for generations now are ready to take things to the next level. They are anxious to perpetrate their ungodly plans for America and the rest of the world, and they are getting weary from waiting.

One "big problem" for them, is a man named "Trump." Perhaps a little more than just your average ordinary man but with a unique and extraordinary call on his life. The good people of this country went to the polls and with God's blessing voted him into office. All the while, behind the scenes, God is also working. He has allowed a reprieve for America, and we are not the only ones!

Everything just stopped one day, someone just put on the brakes, and that someone was God in His infinite MERCY. Trump's election was not supposed to happen. It was against all the odds "maybe some kind of fluke" or surprise to everyone, or was it? I can tell you that many faithful and mature Christians, not all Christians, realized that the election of Trump was some kind of "mission of mercy" perhaps even a "grace period" for the people of God. So, the Church might have more time to prepare!

With our eyes being opened, we must begin to stand as a more unified, more relevant, and more effective Church body than ever before. A "much anticipated light" in this ever-darkening world. It is a reprieve to get our house and our lives in order. We should identify and find our rightful place, beginning with the quickening of many backsliders, and including an all-out "wake-up call" for the world, and the people of God.

I do not want to sound cliché, but it is as if God is sounding a great TRUMPET. God is saying: wake-up, Be alert!! Pay attention! Prepare your house! Get in right standing with Me! It is time to take personal- inventory! it is about what is important to God- that is what should be important to each of us. Time may be one of our most important commodities right now. Where are you right now? Are you prepared for the unknown? Do you have a relationship with God? Does he speak to you? Are your loved ones saved and on and on?

The following are a few scripture verses that apply to our time! Luke 21:34**: "But take heed to yourselves, lest your hearts be weighed down with carousing, drunkenness, and cares of this life, and that day come on you unexpectedly."** Also, Mark 4:19 (GW): **"And the cares of this world, and the deceitfulness of riches, and the lusts of other things entering in, choke the word, and it becometh unfruitful."** Finally, a different version, Mark 4:19 (MSG): **"But are overwhelmed with worries about all the things that have to do and all the things they want to get. The stress strangles what they heard, and nothing comes out of it."** This is a call to get our priorities in order!

PART 1

So, here we are, how the book of Psalms accurately predicted the 2019-2020 and current political landscape of the United States. The following single verse of scripture can be taken in three parts, so I will cover them in order, and one at a time. I believe the last part of this verse, is the most recognizable of the three, so we will save the best for the last!

Psalm 1:1 **says: (1)-"Blessed is the man that walketh not in the counsel of the ungodly, (2)-nor standeth in the way of sinners, (3)-nor sitteth in the seat of the scornful."**

The key to this important verse of scripture is for it to be taken in the context of our modern American political landscape. (1) "... **walketh not in the counsel of the ungodly"** This portion of the verse is referring to not coming into agreement with the agenda and the beliefs of an **ungodly** political entity. Blessed is the man that does not compromise Godly principles.

The **ungodly** here are identified as a people group that do not align themselves with Godly principles- what God considers truth, what God considers righteous, what God has revealed in his Word about living and functioning in a society. This includes what God considers relevant or important Biblical truths and principles. So, rather than walk in the "counsel of the ungodly"- why not walk as the Godly or good man?

Proverbs 2:20 says: **"that thou mayest walk in the way of good men and keep the paths of the righteous."** The ungodly however have their own set of values, principles, and beliefs that are, or become, contrary to the moral values contained in scripture. Where does their rule book come from? Good question! Certainly not from the God of the Bible.

I do not think liberals consider themselves "ungodly." I believe most are simply ignorant of the truth. I am sure many believe that they are doing the right thing. However, the outcome of their actions is not good. One day they need to "see the light." On the other hand, some are fully aware and fully intent on doing evil. That is God's job to sort them out. He will judge all of us at the proper time. For the last verse of Ecclesiastes says: **"For God shall bring every work into judgment, with every secret thing, whether it be good, or whether it be evil."**

When you blow the smoke screen away, when you remove the cloak, or peel back the veil, their brand of morals, their concepts about the world and life in general- are "ungodly"- or not Godlike. The Merriam-Webster dictionary defines ungodly as *"denying or disobeying God, not believing in or respecting God, immoral or evil, contrary to moral law, sinful, wicked."* This just blows me away. This, to me, is shocking because we have been so accustomed to competing and opposing political parties in our electoral process, to the point that it just seems "normal."

But not anymore! No, times have changed. I tell you the Kingdom of God is coming. Remember Isaiah saying, "the vile shall no longer be called liberal." As I said before, they no longer have the privilege of operating and functioning in the dark with a false cloak of morality. Just like in Isaiah, they have been exposed. God now calls them out, yet this time he labels them as "ungodly!"

I, myself, do not want to receive that identification from God. Let us be among those that understand these things. In the end, it does not go well with the ungodly or unrepentant sinners or the wicked for that matter. Ecclesiastes 8:13, says, **"but it shall not be well with the wicked: neither shall he prolong his days, which are as a shadow, because he feareth not before God."** Oftentimes, God allows sinners to come to the full manifestation of their ungodliness before He pronounces judgment upon them.

Ecclesiastes 8:11, says, **"because sentence against an evil work is not executed speedily, therefore the hearts of the sons of men is fully set in them to do evil."**

The Lord commands us here to not walk or function or have anything to do with these organizations. These ungodly, **walk in the counsel** together, this counsel I am referring to is where the governing bodies, and law makers, gather to form their opinions, draft legislation, and vote on policy. Yes, I am singling out, LIBERAL law makers.

Concerning the use of the term, "counsel," I cover in more depth and with better understanding in Part 2 of this chapter. So, I only briefly cover it here. These liberal law makers function within what we commonly know as the Democratic party. This should no longer be the case, they should no longer "freely function" under the banner of democracy. Truthfully, they would more appropriately be labeled, as the "godless party."

If you are a Christian and find yourself in the liberal Democratic party, you have quite a dilemma my friend. Do the ultra-liberal views mirror your own beliefs and values? If you are a Christian and register to vote as a Democrat, how can you agree or <u>walk</u> with values God condemns? It would be a good time to step back and examine yourself and your standing in the light of scripture. Amos 3:13 says: **"Can two walk together, except they be agreed?"**

Back to the Psalms, the second part of Verse 1, says: (2) **"nor standeth in the way of sinners."** Remember! Staying with the political narrative. Now, do not read this as someone standing in the way- <u>blocking or obstructing sinners</u>- that is not the case. A better understanding would be, nor standeth in the way <u>with them</u>- this is the proper definition- in the way with- and not in the way of-!!! So in other words, do not include yourself among their ranks, do not join in their ways, and do not agree with their policies.

Psalm 1:1, "nor standeth in the way of sinners."

Remember, as before, to apply this verse in the context of our nation's political landscape. So, this verse is almost a photo or snapshot of a man or woman, standing in a line at the polls, and waiting their turn to cast their vote. According to these scriptures, their "vote" is considered a <u>godly act</u> or <u>ungodly act</u>, based entirely on their <u>agreement</u> or <u>dis-agreement</u> with Biblical principles!

I have yet to go to an election in this country and not have to <u>stand</u> in a line, what an precise description. These "sinners" are not aligning themselves with Godly morals or just principles. They are referred to as sinners because they have yet to repent of their sins before God. When a man becomes "saved" he is acknowledging his sinful ways and therefore repents of all wrongdoing. It is faith in (Jesus Christ) Gods son, that changes you on the inside, from a sinner to a saint.

I tell you, these sinners are in need of a Savior!- "Oh God, open their eyes and draw them to Yourself," and in the meantime, I will stand in the election line for Your truth. It is a political and moral issue! That is heavy! It literally reads like someone, <u>standing in the wrong line or standing on the wrong issues</u>.

God's laws are just. Himself, as Creator of all things, allows Himself the privilege to determine what is right and what is wrong. His wisdom is far above what man can fathom. We, as men and woman, need to find what those issues are and faithfully follow them. This helps bring us in right standing with God. It is our duty. It is also a great honor and our privilege, to know and understand the truth! We must realize God has already provided us with the rule book.

Proverbs 4:14 says: **"enter not into the path of the wicked and go not in the way of evil men."** When Psalms says: **"standeth in the way"** as we discussed earlier, Proverbs reinforces the Psalm with, **go not in the way.** Where Psalms says **sinners**- Proverb says, **evil men.** These verses "definitely support" each other and show a common theme among the books of the Bible.

Notice the end of Verse 1, that is, Psalm 1:1: (3) **"nor sitteth in the seat of the scornful"** – This final part of verse 1 is the "most prophetic" out of the three. Again, this speaks of coming into union or joining with beliefs and ideals contrary to righteous ones. Do not sit with them. Do not politically support them. The wording for **scornful** used in this context is an exact representation of a political event that may have been seen by literally millions in this nation, and I'm quite sure, many people abroad as well.

The word described as scornful or scorn is defined by Merriam-Webster dictionary as an *"open dislike and disrespect, or mockery, often mixed with indignation."* And mockery is defined as *" insulting or contemptuous action or speech."* Remember, this event must be viewed in the context of our modern American political landscape

On February 4, 2020 was the State of the Union address. As goes the event, the President stands at the podium and gives a speech on the state of the union as instructed in our Constitution.

As goes, the Vice President and the Speaker of the House remain **seated** behind the President except for periodic moments of applause. Pelosi, current Speaker of the House, is considered the third ranking member, in a succession, designed to replace our President if he became unable to fulfill his duties. This is a high office in our government, including broad influence in todays' Democratic Party.

Psalm 1:1: **"nor sitteth in the seat of the scornful."** At this event- Speaker of the House, Nancy Pelosi- was seated to the left hand of the President. Just prior to Trump's last words, Nancy Pelosi can be seen sitting behind the President in what appeared to be a "trial run ripping motion." She then abruptly stands to her feet and rips her copy of President Donald Trump's speech in half, leaving it on her desk in full view for everyone to see! Notice the word "seated" or the King James version, **sitteth.** So, what about the **"seat of the scornful"?**

Psalm 1:1: "nor sitteth in the seat of the scornful."

I would have to say that anyone who watched the 2020 State of the Union address would likely never forget it. It could not have been more public, including a large viewing audience, it is now even being called by some as "the rip that was heard around the world." It was a blatant, open and public display of the term **scornful:**

Dictionary.com defines scorn as**:** *"to treat or regard with contempt or disdain"* and once again, Merriam-Websters**,** *"open dislike and disrespect..."* (which once again, is the very definition of scornful). How could it be that the scriptures are this accurate down to the last details?

If you have yet to discover the beauty and wonder of God's Word, what are you waiting for? We are still not done! One year earlier, during the 2019 State of the Union address, Pelosi again seated behind the President, stands to her feet, and in this case, Pelosi can be seen applauding the President in a mocking type gesture- again in full view of the public.

Mockery: "insulting or contemptuous action..."

This was indeed a disrespectful and insulting act! The word mockery, taken from the Merriam-Webster definition of "scorn" would be defined as, *"insulting or contemptuous action or speech."* I just cannot think of a better word or words to describe Speaker of the House Pelosi's blatant disregard for the position of the President.

Pelosi is a diehard liberal, whom many consider the most powerful woman in politics and representative of today's ultra-liberal Democratic party. She is a face for the movement and holds a distinct role in our government. That also means she needs to be held accountable and to a higher standard than many others.

One final note, the term "scorn" in our culture has historically been used to describe a female. Maybe you have heard the phrase, **"hell hath no fury but a woman scorned."** Also, Pelosi is the first female to serve as Speaker of the House.

I tell you it is time to wake up for this scripture truly "speaks of our time"! The next verse, that is Psalms, chapter 1, Verse 2, addresses the other side of the argument. Rather than continue to describe what we should NOT do, this verse tells us what we should be doing instead: We all need to open our <u>Bibles</u> and <u>follow the instructions</u>!!!- Psalm 1:2: **"but whose delight is in the law of the LORD, and who mediates on His law day and night."** I tell you this is how you transform your life! Whether you're the president of the United States, or your stuck in some prison cell. God is your answer!

PART 2

So, the full text for Part 2-is as follows: and I have divided them into (nine) parts- Psalm 2:1-4: (1) **"Why do the heathen (2) rage, (3) and the people imagine a vain thing? (4) The kings of the Earth (5) set themselves, and the rulers (6) take counsel together, (7) against the Lord, and against His anointed, saying, (8) Let us break their bands asunder, and cast away their cords from us. (9) He that sitteth in the heavens shall laugh: The Lord shall have them in derision."**

Psalms 2:1: (1) "**Why do the heathen rage**"- the term heathen defined in the Google Dictionary as, *"a person regarded as lacking culture or moral principles"* and Dictionary.com as, *"a people that do not acknowledge the God of the Bible."* Here we are again, the Bible is consistent, just another description of the terms, liberal, vile, and ungodly. These words can pretty much be used interchangeably.

Here, the heathen become "enraged." (2) Rage is good term to describe the words, thoughts, attitudes, and actions of Trump haters. The Google Dictionary defines rage as a, *"aggressive behavior or violent anger caused by a stressful or frustrating situation."* Certainly, the liberals are stressed and frustrated with Trump's tenure as President. It appears they will not be able to rest until Trump is no longer in the White House, a sad but all too true reality.

(3) "**And the people imagine a vain thing**"-again these people taken in context are political and they participate in elections. This verse reminds me of the preamble to our Constitution of the United States *"We the people."* Yet, in this case the verse is again referring to the liberal political party. We also need to include the

preamble of the United Nations as follows, *"We the people of the United Nations determined..."*

Next, the people imagine **a** <u>vain</u> thing. The definition of the word imagine in the Google Dictionary can mean *"to believe in (something unreal or untrue) as being true."* So, for just for one example, how about the mass hysteria surrounding climate change? I would say if you believe mankind must take immediate and drastic actions so as to "save our planet," then this would fit well within that definition as *"unreal or untrue"* Quick note: I have tried to build a strong (scriptural) case against climate change "hysteria" in chapter 5.

Next, "a **vain thing**." Our word for <u>vain</u> again under Google Dictionary can mean *"having an excessive opinion of one's own abilities."* So, one, these people believe in something that is not true (hysteria surrounding climate change) and two, they have an inflated opinion of their ability to solve the problem. There are those who think they are somehow going to save the planet, an *"excessive opinion"* of their *"ability"* and I tell you, you have more important things to do which I talk about later.

Again, please humble yourself. God is not calling us to panic! God Almighty Himself has everything under control. What is important to God is our right standing with Him. He makes provision in the future concerning our Earth's environment, which He made by His own power therefore man's efforts are futile.

Back to the main point, the same dictionary describes vain as *"producing no result, useless."* Both definitions seem to work well in this context. For the latter definition describes any likely outcome of the people, apart and separate from God's own will and purpose. This would include man-kinds overall vain and ungodly attempts to forge ahead with any kind of future government, that does not include, the Bible, His principles, His statutes and eternal rulership. Yes, I am talking about our Lord God Almighty Himself. It is vanity brother I mean it is vanity!

Here in Psalms chapter 2-verse 2: we see, (4) **"The kings of the Earth"** So the term for <u>kings</u> here can refer to their political positions. While the use of the term, <u>earth</u> can refer to their global or world-wide range of influence. The verse goes on to say, **"The kings of the Earth-(5) set themselves"** Additionally, the term <u>set themselves</u> or a better Hebrew translation would be "present themselves" **this** would describe being a "re-present-ative." So, here, when taken together we have a global or world-wide body of political representatives, so this is a very precise description of what is commonly known today as–the "United Nations." That is, the U.N. as a whole and even more specifically in this case, the U.N. "General Assembly".

The United Nations was formed and came into being in 1945 with the signing of the official U.N. Charter. This was done on June 26th in the city of San Francisco. This is coincidentally, the hometown of Congresswoman and Madam Speaker of the House, Nancy Pelosi. This General Assembly meets yearly in September at the United Nations Headquarters in New York. There are currently 193 member states, all of whom provide their own representatives. They serve under many titles, including Presidents, Prime Ministers, and as the verse describes, <u>kings or rulers.</u> As with many nations, (in similarity to the U.S.) our President appoints or nominates a representative known as an "Ambassador." The title of Ambassador can simply mean an "official representative." Again, aligning with the scripture, set themselves.

Together they go about the business of international and global affairs. In this forum they freely discuss and strategize, or <u>take counsel</u> on, their guiding principles set forth in the Charter of the United Nations.

Interestingly, the verse: '' (6) **take counsel together**'' has another meaning in the Strong's Concordance definition, it can also mean to *"sit down together."* Wouldn't you know that on the U.N. website, among the opening pages, they go on to describe their unique seating protocol as follows, *"sitting arrangements in the General Assembly Hall change for each session. During the 74th session (2019-2020) Ghana occupies the first seat in the Hall-followed by all the other countries, in English alphabetical order."*

Psalm 2:2: "The kings of the Earth set themselves
and the rulers take counsel together."

Psalm 1:1: "Walketh not in the counsel of…"

If you were to walk the halls of the U.N. building, you would be able to view portraits of both present and former General Secretariats. Again the U.N. is a primary source of liberal theology. This **take counsel together** is repeated and is the same **counsel** described in Psalm 1:1 as **"walketh not in the counsel of the ungodly."** Article 13 of the U.N. Charter lists the following quote *"the General Assembly shall initiate studies and make recommendations concerning International cooperation in the political field. Also, in the areas of economic, social, cultural, educational, and health fields."*

So, here we have a global body where members can take counsel together and based on the few quotes' they have plenty to talk about. Next, (7) **"against the Lord, and against His anointed."** So, here we get to the bottom of the "real motivation" behind the U.N. global body. Yes, they will not just come out officially and confirm it!

But SECRETLY they have no plans on promoting the true Christian religion or adhering to Biblical values. No, rather they promote tolerance or just another code word for anti-Christian theology. Although they likely may support some liberal, deceptive and misleading interpretation of the Bible. They ultimately are <u>against the Lord</u>. So instead of taking an official stance against Christianity, rather they devise ways of cloaking their true intentions.

One way of defending their benevolent reputation is with the careful use of separate global organizations, such as, The World Council of Religious Leaders which is self-described as, *"an independent body, works to bring religious resources to support the work of the United Nations."*

Let me tell you these liberal kings and rulers or leaders are not sitting around basing their studies and recommendations on the study of scripture. They are not arriving at their conclusions after seeking the God of the Bible with petitions and prayerful consideration. Rather, to the contrary, the verse says they are against the Lord and against His anointed. And, might I add, against conservative Christians, as well as our current sitting President.

The King James version says: (8) **"Let us break their bands asunder and cast away their cords from us."** For a better understanding I have provided the following Bible verses of Psalms 2:3 (CSB)- Holman Christian Standard Bible: **"Let us tear off their chains and free ourselves from their restraints."** (GNT)- Good News Translation: **"Let us free ourselves from their rule, they say; let us throw off their control."** These verses of scripture best describe the deliberate, conscience, and careless decision to renounce Christ and genuine Christianity including Biblical restraints, safeguards, laws, and statutes. God indeed has given mankind detailed instructions on how to live a blessed life. I will mention again, 2 Timothy 3:16 which says: **"All scripture is given** by inspiration of God, and is profitable for doctrine, for reproof, for correction, for instruction in righteousness."

Next, chapter 2:4: says (9) "**He that sitteth in the heavens shall laugh, the Lord shall have them in derision.**" Here we see a sovereign God that sitteth in the heavens. In other words, He (God) is so far above man-kinds vain and even laughable attempts to form another world government that is separate from God. Don't they learn anything? Therefore, just as they scorned or mocked God's man in the office of the President and including those Christians who voted for and supported him, and all those who keep his principles, He too in return shall have them in derision. So, He ultimately one day will cause them to become objects of scorn, ridicule, and mockery themselves.

Now, finally, skipping down to Verse 10 "**be wise therefore, o ye kings: be instructed ye judges of the earth. Serve the Lord with fear.**" True to His character, God gives another alter call, or God can be seen reaching out to these kings and judges of the Earth. This is a call to repentance. This is an invitation to connect with God and do things His way. You know! You have heard the phrase, "It's my (His) way or the HIGHWAY." Matthew 7:13 (NLT): "**You can enter God's kingdom only through the narrow gate. The highway to hell is broad and it's gate is wide for the many who choose that way.**"

What road or what path are you on? Brothers or sisters, it is time to make that assessment. I encourage you to get on your knees, that is the most powerful place anyone could go, and call out to God, that is the most powerful thing anyone could do! Amen.

Proverb 1:6: "To understand a proverb, and the interpretation:
the words of the wise, and their dark sayings."

5

Wisdom And Warnings

Proverbs and other verses

For the full text of the book of Proverbs, covered here- see chapter 1- verses 1-6 and 22-33. In this chapter, I will use a somewhat easier to understand and modern version of the Bible that is "God's Word" or (GW) version. So, the (GW) version will apply to the Book of Proverb's verses unless otherwise indicated. In Proverbs chapter 1, Verse 1: **"The Proverbs of Solomon, David's son who was King of Israel."** A "proverb" can be defined as *"a brief popular saying that gives advice about how people should live or that expresses a belief that is generally thought to be true."* So, let us go through some "foundational" verses found in chapter 1. These verses describe wisdom in all its various forms, all of which contain the power to develop Godly character.

Starting with verse 2: **"to grasp wisdom and discipline."** Wisdom is what Solomon asked God for, for the purpose of leading and governing his people. Wisdom comes from God and is vital information according to God. "Discipline" is a product of "wisdom." It takes discipline to become a mature believer in Christ. We must read, study, and pray God's Word if we expect to be a successful Christian.

"**To understand deep thoughts**"- oftentimes, contained in scripture are "deep truths" that are not always recognizable at first glance. This is not the case with ordinary books, yet the Word of God is written by God Almighty. Hidden within the text, God often reveals additional profound meanings which can be especially important and significant at that time to the seeker.

Verse 3: "**to acquire the discipline of wise behavior**"- here, there is no excuse, God reveals that "with Him" we have been given the ability to "acquire" and regularly function in "wise behavior" including "righteousness and justice and fairness." It is God's desire that His people walk in "wise behavior" and similar attributes, both in our personal as well as professional lives. This is particularly vital for those who are in authority. People in government have the potential to affect millions of lives based upon day to day activities. We, as a people, need daily wisdom. God is not honored when we only attend church on Christmas and Easter, do not deceive yourselves.

Verse 4: "**to give insight to gullible people.**" The word "gullible" means "easily deceived or cheated." Wow! This verse is powerful. You mean studying our Bibles will make us difficult to deceive, or unable to be cheated?! This is the root cause of liberal and global politicians' worst fears that is of the scriptures, and of the Christians, because we as dedicated and loyal Christians know the truth. They are "betting on" the masses to be ignorant, uninformed, and easily deceived, right! So, no matter how many times they repeat the lie, we are not buying it!

Verse 4: "**to give knowledge and foresight to the young.**" It is important to God that we teach our children scripture, especially in these days. They are bombarded with highly deceptive and well-crafted lies and propaganda. Really- you can only fight back armed with the truth! The futures of our precious children are at stake. We must not neglect, nor fail, to educate the young. This is a big problem in our nation, and we must do a better job. Currently, the liberals, the ungodly, are winning this effort and things need to change! It is far easier to influence their minds while they are still young. The Bible says in Proverbs 22:6 (KJV): **"Train up a child the way he should go and when he is old, he will not depart from it."**

Verse 5: **"A wise person will listen and continue to learn."** This is an attribute of a "wise person"- the ability to "listen" and continue to "learn." You should never stop learning. My mother read books every day, even throughout her eighties, and her mind was sharp right up to the end.

Has anyone noticed how Donald Trump frequently gathers experienced leaders and people of expertise for roundtable dis-cussions on various political, business, or professional issues? He has trained himself to habitually "listen." This is an attribute of a wise leader. Proverbs 1:5 (KJV): **"A wise man will hear and will increase learning; and a man of understanding shall attain unto wise counsels."** Trump has consistently shown his ability to continue to "increase learning"- even as new issues come to the forefront.

"And an understanding person will gain direction." I tell you, one of the greatest benefits I have enjoyed since becoming a Christian would be the ability to receive "direction" for my life. This nearly entails every aspect of my personal, business, and day to day life decisions that I can now make with the utmost confi-dence. If you do not have that level of relationship with Almighty God, you are missing out!

As far as politics go, direction is indispensable. What if Clinton had Godly direction in the 1990's when dealing with foreign policy, and particularly China, a real problem today. What if the Supreme Court had Godly direction, every time they heard a case? What if our President had access to Godly direction on a regular basis? You know, misinformed and gullible people pay good money to get false direction from psychics, tarot card readers, horoscopes, spirit guides, or other occultic sources- an all too sad reality in our world. God wants us to come to Him. God wants us to seek Him and God is willing to direct and guide our lives for our good. John 16:13 (KJV): **"Howbeit when He, the Spirit of Truth, is come, He will guide you into all truth."**

Next, verse 6: **"to understand a Proverb and a clever saying, the words of wise people and their riddles."** This verse reminds me of Luke 8:10 (KJV): Jesus said, **"unto you it is given to know the mysteries of the Kingdom of God, but to others in parables, that seeking they might not see, and hearing they might not understand."** The Lord "has the abilities" to give us "understanding" of His written Word, even revealing "hidden knowledge"- not unlike clever sayings and riddles!

He has not given this wisdom to the "ungodly." A man must humble himself before Almighty God and therefore qualify for divine insight into hidden truths found in His Word. Therefore, Jesus came speaking in "parables." Contained in scripture are certain truths that God has reserved for those that are His. And for those that are not, they have not been given the ability to understand. A parable is defined as a short story or allegory used to illustrate or teach some important truth, religious principle, or moral lesson.

Verse 6: **"The fear of the Lord is the beginning of knowledge."** Really, the "fear of the Lord" is a term used to describe the proper relationship between "God and man." This fear is often described as "respect." However, this "fear of the Lord" is also a genuine fear and knowing that He alone possesses the ability to judge and punish us, if needed and when required. This "fear" is reserved for God and God alone! So please take **WARNING**. In Matthew 10:28 (KJV): Jesus said, **"and fear not them which kill the body, but are not able to kill the soul, but rather fear Him which is able to destroy both soul and body in hell."**

Hell is real my friend! And you do not want to go there, neither do you want to "gamble" with eternity. You do not want to "roll the dice" and hopefully make it to Heaven. A devout follower of God can have assurance and be confident in their salvation. Hell is so god-awful the human mind is hardly able to conceive of the horrors. A man's denial of its existence cannot change its reality. Hell's punishment, as portrayed early in Genesis 4:13 KJV: **"And Cain said to the LORD, my punishment is greater than I can bear."**

Let me tell you, everyone in hell is suffering in a capacity beyond their ability to cope with it and this is by design. The Lord also said in Mathew 18:9 (KJV): **"And if thine eye offend thee, pluck it out, and cast it from thee: it is better for thee to enter into life with one eye, rather than having two eyes to be cast into hell fire."**

I believe men and women would be shocked if they knew the true number of our past "well known personalities, popular celebrities, and cultural icons" who are not in Heaven today. Oh God, please help us all Amen! Additionally, the "fear of God" helps us to be and remain in good standing with Him. Proverbs 16:6 (KJV): ..."**by the fear of the Lord men depart from evil.**" So, in proper relationship with God Almighty, we then qualify for many great and hopeful promises; for example, Psalms 37:11 (KJV): **"But the meek shall inherit the earth; and shall delight themselves in the abundance of peace."**

Verse 6: **"stubborn fools despise wisdom and discipline."** Sadly, many people rebel against God. Far too many people develop inaccurate thoughts or feelings towards God, apart from the Bible and without any real basis in truth. Some blame God for every wrong in their life and stubbornly resist any argument contrary to their own beliefs.

You can get away with this behavior for a while however, eventually, one day, you will be confronted with the reality. Trust me when I say, every atheist who has ever died is today a believer in Christ. The scripture says in James 2:19 (KJV): **"Thou believest that there is one God! Though doest well; the devils also believe and tremble."**

Even the "devils" who are contrary to God do not want you to acknowledge the truth, yet they themselves know full well of His sovereign credentials and indeed "tremble."

Now, let us skip down to chapter 1, verse 22: **"How long will you gullible people love being so gullible? How long will you mockers find joy in your mocking? How long will you "fools" hate knowledge?"** "How long" says the Lord- three times for emphasis. Here, the Good Lord is found pleading with the people or these lost souls saying, "how long will you refuse vital knowledge that can transform your life? How long will you not follow me? How long will you walk contrary to sound wisdom?" This is but a small display of God's patience and longsuffering towards man.

Verse 23: **"Turn to me when I warn you"** and **"you did not want me to warn you."** What a travesty. Could there be a scenario where God attempted to warn a person, ruler, or President, maybe of some important decision or impending danger that may require prompt reaction or response? This verse goes deep in territory not often well known or discussed.

One recent example of this verse took place when President Trump quickly and decisively closed travel from China amid the Covid-19 outbreak, contrary to the prevailing thoughts and opinions of so-called experts and authorities, including the World

Health Organization. This quick action by Trump surely slowed the spread of the disease in this country.

Could you just imagine the same scenario under the leadership of a liberal and politically correct leader? That is, void of wisdom, and without common sense or reliance on God! This is but a small example. Could you imagine a split-second decision surrounding nuclear weapons- a potentially far greater destructive ability- an area with enormous implications?

Numerous times in the Bible have men responded, or not responded, according to God's warnings. Typically, you must know God and His Word, or need to depend on others that do. As sitting President, this goes with the territory— this goes with the job description— particularly, "Commander and Chief." From time to time, God will lead His people out of and far from dangers of all kinds. I, for one, want to hear and perceive God's warnings in every area of life.

Verse 24: **"I called, and you refused to listen."** verse 25: **"I stretched out my hands to you, and no one paid attention. You ignored all my advice**." How many advisors do you think someone has in Trump's position? Hopefully, persons in leadership have good, sound advisors and experts. What about God's advice? Many people would not think of God that way- as a God that wants to communicate with His people, first, through His Word, and secondly, by His Holy Spirit.

Are you aware that God may be talking to you? Perhaps He has called you. Maybe He is **"stretching out His hands to you"** or maybe He would like to give you **"advice"** on some issue. I do not want to **"ignore"** God's advice. We may not even know the repercussions of failing to discern God's voice.

We all make decisions every day. Not every decision carries a weighty response; however, from time to time people make decisions that could change the course of their life. How much more a President or leader that may affect entire nations?

Brother, I want God's advice and the good news is that He is willing to communicate with us. In these verses, you get a sense of God pleading, pursuing, and desiring to bring clarity. He also is desiring to have relationships and two-way communications. He wants to build an understanding of the things of God in for our lives. We can see Him making the effort. He is the one calling. He is the one reaching out.

Will you or will you not respond to His repeated calls? Do not refuse to listen as in verse 24. Pay attention. Do not ignore God's advice on a practical level. That depends on where you are with God. It may simply mean reading your Bible, praying, and going to church. For others, it may require even more interaction with God based on experience.

You know, God successfully communicated to hundreds of His people on 9/11 in New York's Twin Towers. Many lives were spared from that destruction. Yet how many did not receive His warnings? It was real- the vital and important relationship with God really mattered to many on that day. It is wisdom to know and be acquainted with God and His Word if you are not already.

Verse 26: "**I will laugh at your calamity.**" verse 27: "**when panic strikes you, when calamity strikes you, when trouble and anguish come to you.**" verse 28: "**they will call to me at that time, but I will not answer. They will look for me, but they will not find me.**" This is a frightening scripture. I certainly do not want to be in this place after repeated attempts by God to get someone's attention, God's calling out, to put them on the right path in life, to bring correction, healing and deliverance, wholeness and truth, to teach men and women His ways and to become in "right standing" with God.

He will not call out forever. Eventually, a person needs to heed and respond and obey the promptings and callings of God. Here, God uses some heavy language to describe a person's rejection of the truth. They "hated" knowledge and they "despised" His warnings. Verse 29: **"because they hated knowledge and did not choose the fear of the Lord."** verse 30: **"They refused my advice. They despised my every warning."** Eventually, God will stop calling out to the person who continues to reject His words and refuses to acknowledge Him as the source of all wisdom.

Verse 31: **"they will eat the fruit of their lifestyle."** God will let them have their own way and bear the consequences involved. How many of you would like to experience living without worry? I have no doubt, millions are living under some level of stress or worry even daily. We humans seem to love to worry about something or everything. It does not make sense to worry about something you cannot change.

I credit God for teaching me to live free from worry, stress and fears over things that are beyond my control. The Lord wants us to cast our cares on him. How many doctors write prescriptions every day- symptoms caused by the epidemic of worry, stress, and fear are so prevalent in society? Do not ever forget God's promises! Move on with God and expect good things.

Verse 33: **"but whoever listens to me will live without worry and will be free from the dread of disaster"** with practical experience and a growing relationship with God. I believe God is watching and He cares about our choices. 1 John 3:22 (KJV): **"Whatsoever we ask, we receive of Him; because we keep His commandments and do those things that are pleasing in His sight."**

I hope this book puts you on a right path with God, for yourself, your children, and your loved ones- including this beloved country of ours. With God's help, we are going to make it. Whatever the future holds, we will be prepared, we will be able to handle it, and we will not be ignorant nor caught off guard. Put your faith in Christ and you can never lose! Amen!

6

Seven Issues

Introduction

S o, here we are, one important purpose of this book. That is, to help instruct people in the ways of wisdom, that is, in the ways of God. We can no longer afford to rely on our own understanding. We should not be adopting as truth persons random opinions, philosophies, or earthly wisdom of men (remember, the counsel of the ungodly or counsel apart or separate from God)

We should instead place our trust in the ultimate source of wisdom and knowledge that is by humbling ourselves under the hand of Almighty God. To seek His wisdom, His laws, and His principles to guide our every thought and every action.

Also, it is important to realize that we are at a moment in history where the consequences of our decisions are magnified because of the prophetic implications of our day. The very real fact that God is revealing things about our world today more than ever before, lends to the fact that we are indeed in a unique time. What we think, say, and do is more important now than ever before.

If you or your loved ones are struggling with these words, I want to take a moment for those who have not yet received the Lord Jesus Christ as your personal Savior. I say "do it now"- do not hesitate, it only takes one moment. The scripture says in Romans 10:9: **"If you confess with your mouth the Lord Jesus and believe in your heart that GOD has raised Him from the dead, ye shall be saved."** Just simply follow the "instruction manual."

I would like to tell you- I was a sold out liberal in my thinking and beliefs until I got saved and renewed my mind with the truths found within the pages of the Bible. In general, the Bible supports conservative values, while at the same time condemning liberal ones. What side of this equation are you on? If your delight is on the law, commandments, doctrines, and principles in scripture, then you are in a good place. If you spend time meditating on God's laws, as the Lord instructs us daily- then you are in a great place!

Daily time in His Word helps us to triumphantly overcome life's many challenges. Consistent daily time in His Word also builds our faith and level of maturity.

Psalm 119:105 says: **"It is like a light unto your path and direction for your life."** And this includes many great promises in His Word that we may claim, believe, and apply to our own lives as well. That is for your sons and daughters also.

There are promises for protection, healing, deliverance, prosperity, eternal life, and much, much more. And lastly, I want to mention the incredible power of prayer which is another sometimes misunderstood or unappreciated benefit of becoming a Christian.

Also, allow me to stress the fact that a person's conservative values do not get them saved. It is faith in God alone that gets you saved. Do not put your political values, either conservative or liberal, before God or to replace God. God says in the Ten Commandments- **"Though shalt have no other GOD before Me."**

God, family, and country is a good order of things for our lives. I confess that I am often tempted to put politics before family. It can be difficult when your loved ones are on opposite sides politically. Yet, it may take much prayer, including consistent prayer over long periods may sometimes be required. Never give up, your sincere faithful prayer would never be in vain, it certainly is far more important that loved ones are saved than how they vote in the next election.

In fact, as was my case, it was only after my conversion that I began to gain knowledge and come to understand and acknowledge the many evils in our world around me. Some of these include unrestricted abortion, same sex marriage, extreme environmentalism, the morally challenged entertainment industry, anti-Christian world government, irresponsible non-enforcement of our immigration laws, the fake news industry, and the denial of God's rightful place in our culture, schools, and government, etc.

So, it was not until I became well versed in the scriptures that I was well capable of discerning good from evil, including its influences, suddenly all too apparent in my everyday life.

When it comes to discernment, some things should be obvious, like murder for example. I think we all would agree that if someone were to commit a murder, that would be an act that would warrant some measure of justice, including prison time, it may even warrant the ultimate form of justice that is the death penalty. Of course, conservatives and liberals would not have too hard of a time with that.

Yet, at what point do you begin to call abortion "murder," and most importantly, what does the Bible have to say about it? So, I have included abortion as the first and foremost topic of

importance under "issues," among the short list of highly significant issues.

Obviously, there are an infinite number of issues facing our
society these days, however I chose seven of what I feel are the
defining issues of our time. The outcome of these seven will chart
the course and give recognizable clues as to the likely future of
our cherished American way of life. For good or bad, all those
issues of lesser importance, I prefer to leave them up to the politicians themselves.

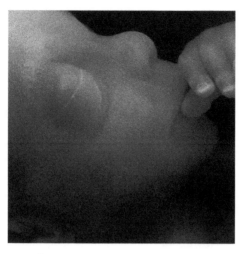

Proverbs 14:21:"...and his children shall have a place of refuge."

ABORTION ON DEMAND

Most of us possess the ability to recognize right from wrong. Yet, when it comes to the "murder" of innocent life in the womb of a woman, incredibly, that blurs the lines for people. It is no longer a matter of common sense for some. I believe if you have a heartbeat, you have a life. It becomes a debate among politicians and judges alike.

It should be clear to everyone, but it depends on where you get your beliefs. For me, there is no debate. It is darkness, vile, and wicked, and like we read in the Psalms- **"ungodly!"**

By casting your ballot, you are becoming complicit and guilty of innocent blood. The Bible is clear on the subject. Psalm 106:38 says: **"and shed innocent blood, even the blood of their sons and of their daughters, whom they sacrificed unto the idols of Canaan: and the land was polluted with blood."**

Also, Deuteronomy 19:10 reads: **"That innocent blood be not shed in thy land, which the LORD thy God giveth thee for an inheritance, and so blood be upon thee."** So, you see, God warns us about abortion, it appears that it may have an effect, on the "**land**." So, abortion may bring a curse, even a stronghold for further demonic activity. Abortion can also directly "effect" the people involved, **"so blood be upon thee,"** I don't think that's going to turn out well. Of course, God can forgive all those involved if they're willing to repent.

It is easy to march in the streets holding a banner for pro-choice, such an innocent, innocuous term to describe abortion. Yet, how many of you, if you had the ability to "see" with your spiritual eyes and look upon a mountain of over sixty million aborted "fetuses"- as the liberals like to call them- it should be a literal mountain of sixty millions reasons to take a stand for pro-life.

If you could look on this scene of unborn children in various stages of development since the 1973 Supreme Court ruling of "Roe vs. Wade"- would you not be appalled? How many would be sick? How many would reconsider? And how many would keep and protect their womb, their baby, both men and women included?

This reminds me of a scripture in Luke 1:41 when a pregnant Elizabeth heard the voice of her cousin Mary, **" ...the baby leaped in her womb."** This verse sounds more like a living child than some throw away, meaningless, and inconvenient tissue. The baby seemed conscience and aware of his surroundings, outside of his mother's body. This verse supports the idea of the womb being sacred and should be protected at all costs.

In another verse, Isaiah 49:1: ..."**the LORD hath called me from the womb: from the bowels of my mother hath he made mention of my name."** This sounds a little like predestination to me. That is the belief that God has foreordained our destinies and even callings in life. So, you will never know, this side of heaven, what any "particular life" may be!

I have also seen women who have had an abortion, have great difficulty physically having children later in life. Most women and men of good conscience regret that decision later in life as well. Why not see this issue through Gods eyes? In Psalms 127:3 the Lord views it from a different angle: **"lo, children are a heritage of the LORD: and the fruit of the womb is his reward."** So, children are indeed of value and life is precious; we must become a society that promotes "life mindedness," we must protect and care for human life.

Have you heard the phrase, "from the cradle to the grave," I think the abortionist got it all wrong, it didn't say "from the womb, then directly to the grave." The issue of abortion is the most black and white issue on the ballot. If you claim to be a Christian and vote for a candidate who openly supports abortion on demand, God help you! Were you aware that Nancy Pelosi, is a self-proclaimed "devout Catholic" and yet staunch supporter of Planned Parenthood? What a contradiction.

You cannot possibly be both without outrightly rejecting God's Word of truth. Voting this way is your signature of approval. Abortion may be the most visible issue, the easiest method for determining God's heart on the matter and determining our vote.

I have sensed a tide, as well as growing opposition, desiring to re-visit and to right the wrong of "Roe vs. Wade" and I believe it is coming from the heart of God. I understand a woman should have control over her own body, but abortion has become so tolerable, socially acceptable, routine, and so easily available and without restriction that things must change in the hearts and minds of the people.

It literally has become an abomination, it has become big business, it has dulled the senses and hearts of the American people. It is no longer a shock to anyone. There are alternatives including sex within marriage only, men and women respecting their bodies and one another, there is abstinence, multiple forms of birth control, there is adoption- which could be made more available with care provided free of charge- and I think there may be small number of special circumstances for providing safe abortions as well. I believe we are in a time when we need to take a step in the right direction.

Daniel 1:25: "the streets shall be built again,
and the wall, even in troublous times"

ILLEGAL IMMIGRATION/BORDER WALL

Let us talk about illegal immigration. In the days of the Bible, men oftentimes built walls around their cities for protective purposes. The gates of their cities were guarded and activity in and out was monitored. Our country has many so called "gates." Many are seaports, some are airports, and others are borders with other countries.

It is vital to any nation to provide adequate facilities able to guard and monitor travel through these gates in and out from the points of entry. These entry points are often facilitators of legal trade between countries, yet they are also known to be used as entry points for illegal drugs, human trafficking, and global terrorist ambitions to import weapons of mass destruction across our borders.

These gates to our nation can be used for both good and evil. This is true with nations throughout the world. The Great Wall in China is an ancient example of the perceived need to protect the nation's best interest. A massive building project, deemed vital for the nation's sovereign control, guarding our gates is essential for any sovereign nation.

There is a move to keep our Southern border open to illegal immigration. Of course, this would and has put the American people in greater danger. Open borders increase the flood of illegal drugs coming into our country. By making these drugs cheaper and easier to get, they are slowly eroding and destroying our youth in this country.

With strong borders, these drugs become harder to get, raising the prices, which results in far fewer people trying, experimenting, and getting hooked on drugs- this will also reduce their popularity.

God only knows what, if any, weapons to be used against the American people have or could have entered this country. Authorities do not even know how many illegal immigrants are presently living in this country.

Immigration laws help to enforce legal immigration to manageable numbers based on supply and demand. It is again the global elites that want to force America to open its border to anyone, regardless of legality, criminal background (friend or foe), or evil intentions. This is a dangerous game. Little good will come of this and the potential for great harm is more likely the outcome.

I have personally worked with many great and talented Hispanic persons in my time in the construction field. However, I have also seen the town where I grew up turn into a "no-go zone" where even the police will not patrol because of the danger to them from gang violence and lawlessness- a result of uncontrolled illegal immigration. This should be reason enough to bring to a halt all illegal activity at all our points of entry.

Not only are there physical walls and gates around our cities and countries, the Bible teaches that there are spiritual or unseen barriers as well. Many Christians acknowledged the removal of God's "Hedge of Protection" around America on 9/11/2001, the first major attack on the Homeland since Pearl Harbor, WWII. In fact, this "Hedge of Protection" is completely Biblical.

There's an interesting account captured in the book of Job, chapter 1. It records an interaction and conversation between God and Satan, wherein Satan accuses Job, in an attempt, to bring into question Job's loyalty to God.

Satan alleges that Job's loyalty was conditional and a result of God's rich blessings on his life. He then acknowledges God's protective barrier around Job and tempts God to put Job to the test. Verse 10 (CJB) says: **"You've put a protective hedge around him, his house, and everything he has."**

Satan was unable to afflict or rain down destruction on Job without God's permission; by removing his protective barrier, he was then allowed to attack, steal, and destroy everything Job had except his own life. The (NLT) version describes this barrier as a "wall of protection"- while the (GW) translations use the term, "protective fence."

So, the Lord uses all these common, everyday understandable terms to describe his unseen, invisible, and supernatural protection. Ecclesiastes 10 says: ..."**whoso breaketh a hedge, a serpent shall bite him.**" In this verse, it seems to indicate that one can "break" the hedge, to his own hurt.

I believe our Hedge of Protection on this nation has been compromised, thereby allowing the attack on us of 9/11. It is certainly Biblical for God to protect people and nations, as well as removing His protection over people and nations. Brother, I do not want to knowingly, or unknowingly, do anything to disturb God's "Hedge of Protection" around my family and loved ones, as well as this great nation.

Collectively, our walls and our gates of this nation must be protected at all costs. Trump's wall between the United States and Mexico is a good idea, not a bad one. Liberals foolishly oppose Trump's efforts to build, restore, and strengthen our protection on the Southern border- which perhaps is the best example of a complete failure to support and enforce the laws on the books. If liberals care not about enforcing the immigration laws, I do not think that they would care about the Constitution or the rule of law in general.

The events in Job's life, mentioned earlier, parallel the events of 9/11/2001-World Trade Center terrorist attacks. Many Christians saw the events as a lifting or removing of God's "Hedge of Protection" from America. We have been blessed in this nation to enjoy such peace here in our own homeland.

As in Job's life when God's protection was removed, it immediately opened the door for "hostile enemies" to attack. The first attack was upon Job's servants and livestock. Job 1: 14-17, This was primarily an attack against his <u>economic resources</u> common in Job's time. This was also true in America when planes hit the World Trade Center (Twin Towers)- these were symbols of New York's <u>Financial</u> District and economic prosperity.

While Job was attacked by the **Sabeans**, and later by the **Chaldeans.** Also, the "**By the Edge of the Sword**" again reveals details describing "Hostile" and "Hostile to America"- sworn enemies. The "**Sword**" is notably common to Islam and Al Qaeda who are openly declared enemies of the United States. The Sword is often featured on their flags, statues, and other Islamic symbols.

Job 1:16 (CEB): "...A raging fire fell from the sky and burned up the sheep and devoured the young men."

Job 1:16: ..."**The fire of God is fallen from heaven, and hath burned up the sheep, and the servants, and consumed them, and I am escaped alone to tell thee."**

"**The fire of God is fallen from heaven"** or in the (CEB) version, "A raging fire fell from the sky "- the word "**fire**" in the Strong's Concordance can mean "burning, fiery, flaming, hot"- though written in ancient Hebrew language this perfectly describes a 767 jet airplane, just leaving the airport, each filled with over 9,000 gallons of jet fuel and bursting in a giant fireball upon impact with the World Trade Center sky scrapers.

The term- **fell** or **"fallen"** might describe the debris field produced from the impact and subsequent explosion affecting the entire area, including over one dozen structures near and around the towers. The Hebrew word for "**heaven**" in this verse can simply mean "sky." This can describe the region of the jets' flight pattern and including the uppermost floors of the towers, as well as the ignition point of the explosion. Sky again gives a clearer picture than perhaps the word "heaven"- although heaven can imply religious terminology as to Islam.

Finally: **"there came a great wind from the wilderness and smote the four corners of the house and it fell upon the young men, and they are dead; and I only escaped alone to tell thee."** So, in this case, Job's children died as the result of a hurricane, tornado, or some powered type wind that collapsed the building on top of them. Yet, when the verse describes "smote the four corners"- I cannot help but to see the image in my mind of the Twin Towers, 110 floors, collapsing in an eerie "all four corners at the same time"- floor by floor- in rapid succession to the bottom. Not once, but twice, both towers, in the same manner.

Again, eerily exact terminology from the Bible, a frightening reality in our modern day. **"It fell upon the young men"** tells the story of the victims that were in that building on that day. The greatest number of deaths were not from the passengers of the jets, but from the collapse of the towers with very few survivors. Yet, some did survive and said, "I only escaped alone to tell thee."

I tell you I look at gates, walls, fences, borders, seaports, and airports in a whole new light. These terrorists from 9/11 entered this country through one of our weakened gates or airports. We were not guarding them from our enemies. We were caught off guard with tragic results. We left the gate wide open. We did not monitor proficiently who came or went.

Trump supports strong borders and continually fights to complete the wall at our Southern border. Liberals wants to remove every obstacle or restriction for common sense border security, hoping their illegal votes will ultimately keep them in power.

Revelation 7:9: "...a great multitude, which no man could number, of all nations, and kindreds, and people, and tongues."

OVER POPULATION

This "particular issue" is not something you go around talking about on the campaign trail. Yet it is on the ballot, and yet still, you will never read it on any "candidates" profile. Sometimes you just need to read between the lines to get to the truth. So, is overpopulation a problem?

Well God said in Genesis 1:28 for man to **"be fruitful and multiply."** Although that was a long time ago, I don't think he has presently retracted that statement. God also is "great" at math, and more than capable of calculating the "livable" surface of the Earth as it relates to the growing population.

So, if you believe that overpopulation is an issue of extreme importance, as do liberal minded global elites, then you will go forth looking for ways to solve the issue.

Of course, wide-spread and easily available access to abortion providers would be essential. Also, extreme measures to protect the already compromised environment from the effects of too much human interaction, would as well, be essential.

But, if you took time to read your Bible, you might learn that there is a day when the Earth's population will be almost completely eradicated, unless the Lord would intervene. Also, you would understand that the Earth will go through much devastating destruction- the result of world-wide war, weapons of mass destruction, both man-made and supernatural events, record breaking earthquakes, out of control weather events, famines, plagues, and nearly every other kind of devastation or destruction imaginable.

It is not a pleasant story, yet the Bible predicts these events in advance. Suddenly, the world is not such a nice place. I, for one, am believing God for His supernatural protection and deliverance for myself, my loved ones, and my family.

I do not desire to witness such devastation and destruction, yet if these things are true, why would you want to behave as if they are not? Are you going to change the reality of God's Word? Are you going to call God a liar? Are you able to turn back the Hand of Almighty God? Well, evidently, some think that way. Do not be deceived and do not be counted among them.

So, the globalists believe the Earth would be better suited to the ideal total population of around 500 million or so, of course they consider themselves as being among the fortunate surviving population. What a stark contrast when compared to todays' approximate 7.8 billion and growing population. Again, no problem, for the scriptures foretell in Mark 13:20: **"And except that the Lord had shortened those days, no flesh should be saved, but for the elect's sake, whom he hath chosen, he hath shortened the days."**

It does not get any plainer than that. That is some heavy truth right there. Notice it did not say "unless we all think happy thoughts." That's right, I was once into New Age too and I know all about their lies. Satan might falsely claim that men's thoughts and collective consciousness will have the ability to solve the world's fundamental problems. They think they may perhaps, save the Earth from destruction foretold by the Christians, but don't you fall for it. It is just a lie, right out of the Devil's playbook.

Stand for the truth today. The days are coming when it may be very costly to do so, maybe sooner than we would like to think! Those who follow God sincerely have multiple promises to appropriate for themselves and on behalf of their children. Are some of you beginning to see how faith in God is all encompassing and can potentially affect outcomes in every facet of life? Let us address another controversial debate among politicians and their constituents.

LGBTQ

The LGBTQ community, diversity training, and same sex marriage have become costly to speak out against. The gay lobby has very successfully nearly labeled it a "hate-crime" in America to not accept as "natural" their beliefs or teachings, even as they are in direct opposition to that of Almighty God.

Diversity training, which sounds so noble, is forcing the acceptance of its beliefs and tolerance of the LGBTQ lobby on all Americans without regard to religious beliefs. I believe the Supreme Court decision of June 15, 2015, to legalize same sex-marriage is a slap in the face of Almighty God. Laws upholding traditional marriage, have served this nation well and have clearly been the law of the land since, and long before, this nation's founding.

Who are these people to "declare" and even "legalize" such atrocious behavior! This only goes to further confuse "already confused" innocent children and young adults. These young people should be treated with the utmost care and loving attention from persons with their best well-being in mind.

However, the gay lobby is hostile to Bible believing Christians and would like to remove every reminder of punishment and accountability recorded and noted in scripture. They have chosen a fight that they cannot win. They may even be taking to hell all those they claim to defend or support or care about, particularly those who are still so young and impressionable.

These vulnerable members of society, still with a ray of hope, and in need of Godly counsel and prayer. This would especially be effective coming from those born-again Christians who already have been delivered and brought out of that same lifestyle, combined with great care and compassion.

I for one (against the opinions of the greater Christian majority) believe that people can indeed be born with homosexual tendencies or desires. Not unlike people who may have been born with "genetic" weaknesses for mental illness and other afflictions common to man. What about genetic tendencies from the womb to becoming more susceptible to alcohol or drug addiction. How can one person drink alcohol and still function and another person's entire life center around alcohol addiction? What about people who are "more likely" to commit or lead a life of crime or what about persons who battle sexual addiction?

So, what about a child who "for some unknown reasons" identifies with the opposite sex from their childhood. I do not believe that every fault or weakness or susceptibility to do wrong comes from our environment or up-bringing. Although, I am not claiming that those can certainly have a major effect, of course they do. But I am not going to disagree with some homosexual person who honestly believes and claims they were "born" that way. Who am I to tell them otherwise?

Having said that, the point is that it is not an acceptable "excuse" to continue in wrongdoing. Not when you have God and the Bible. If you are "caught-up" in this lifestyle, do not continue in your sin. Do not listen to those who would seek to change Gods immutable "laws" to somehow make it appear right.

No, if you instead would just humble yourself and let God change and renew your mind. God can ultimately bring you deliverance, restoration and "salvation" Why? Because the Bible teaches that a man can be "born-again" and there is much teaching in the Bible on this subject. If a man continues in his sin, I tell you that is not good! So, we are all in this together. We all need God, his forgiveness and his "redemption." In fact, that "is" the "Gospel."

The Bible records the punishment of entire cities being destroyed as the consequences of unrestrained, unhindered, homosexual "freedom." The Bible says, in Genesis 13:13, **"the men of Sodom were wicked and sinners before the LORD exceedingly."** I am amazed that the Bible records that God could not find 10 righteous in the city. In Genesis 18:32, **"Peradventure ten shall be found there. I will not destroy it for ten's sake."** So, in fact, God did destroy Sodom and is hauntingly depicted in Chapter 19:28, **"And he (Abraham) looked toward Sodom and Gomorrah, and toward all the land of the plain, and beheld, and, lo, the smoke of the country went up as the smoke of a furnace."**

In fact, it was a place of unimaginable, detestable behavior including violent gang rapes as recorded in Chapter 19:4-5 (GNT) version ..."the men of Sodom surrounded the house. All the men of the city, both young and old, were there, they called out to Lot and asked, 'where are the men who came to stay with you tonight? Bring them out to us!' The men of Sodom wanted**

to have sex with them." This is where the forceful, intolerant gay agenda is moving- make no mistake about it- total depravity and the forceful acceptance upon all who would believe contrary.

Even though they make up a minor some estimate 3% segment of society, their agenda is being forced by the powers of darkness upon innocent, good willed, and unsuspected masses. I recall some years back when the Boy Scouts of America were being coerced to accept openly gay leaders in their ranks. This was highly publicized and there was a lot of controversy as you might imagine.

Eventually it just quietly went away. Now, here we are many years later and the Boy Scouts of America are now being sued for allowing sexual predators into the organization to molest children. Therefore, the organization claimed bankruptcy and have been settling claims of their unfortunate victims.

The following three photos perfectly capture the prophetic nature of the Psalms, chapter 12:7-8.

Psalm 12:7 (NLT) "...this lying generation" (FAKE NEWS)

Psalm 12:7 (NLT) "...the wicked strut about" (PRIDE PARADE)

Psalm 12:8 (NLT) "...evil is praised throughout the land." Also, GW translation: "wicked people PARADE about... " (PRIDE PARADE)

The following verse in Psalms really defines the moral decay so prevalent in today's world. Almost like a snapshot or photograph sent through time and with depth of meaning for today's reader, Psalm 12:7-8 (NLT) -the full text says: **"therefore, LORD, we know you will protect the oppressed, preserving them forever from this lying generation, even though the wicked strut about and evil is praised throughout the land."** (GW) translation: **"wicked people PARADE around when immorality increases among Adam's descendants."** (NIV); **"who freely strut about when what is vile is honored by the human race."**

I believe God will continue to cry out to these lost segments of society for He is long suffering and full of grace and tender mercies. Although the day must come when this will eventually and finally reach a level where God's righteous indignation and wrathful judgment against sin can forebear and wait no longer. God's patience and long suffering will no longer tolerate these wicked behaviors.

I would think practicing abstinence from homosexual acts, with God's help, would be a far better choice than suffering the vengeance of eternal fiery judgement? I am also referring to and including all sexual sins of heterosexuals, as well as the sins of adultery and fornication. I confess, I was an adulterer in my first marriage- I was never taught any different. Yet, I do recall my conscience telling me these things were wrong.

God says that adulterers will not go unpunished. Well, sadly my marriage ended in a painful divorce as well as the life changing effect it has on the innocent children involved; and what they're forced to go through. My second marriage, done God's way and not my way, has been tremendously rewarding and there is just no comparison.

Always choose God's way. To learn more details about homosexual sin and what the Bible has to say read the book of Romans chapter 1 for indeed, there is much written on this subject. This subject is nothing new and has been around for thousands of years. Why now are they changing the laws in favor of it? We are called to vigorously resist this agenda and vote in office those which continue to uphold moral decency and Christian-Judeo traditional values in every facet of society.

For God's ways, His commandments and statutes are eternal and never change, neither should we! Hebrews 13:8, declares that: **"Jesus Christ is the same "yesterday, and today, and forever."** We must come together and stand for truth no matter what the cost, for we must fear God rather than man.

Genesis 6:11: "...and the earth was filled with violence"

GUN CONTROL

Has anyone besides myself noticed that mass shootings in public places making headline news almost weekly, have quietly all but disappeared? This again is due to what I believe is one positive effect of and result of righteous leadership. It likely is affected as well, when leaders in high office pray both privately, as well as publicly, to the God of the Bible.

Check for yourself. Under the previous liberal presidential leadership, mass shootings, as well as domestic and foreign terror attacks, remained consistently an all-time, record high and was continually broadcasted on the daily news channels. This was becoming the new normal. This was a time when many cried out for stricter gun controls and was the biased liberal media's political mantra of the day.

Our forefathers, mostly Godly men, had the foreknowledge and wisdom to author the Second Amendment, which gives the legal right for law abiding Americans to keep and bear arms, and this right was not to be infringed upon. This right is based on the idea that we have the God given right to defend our country, our homes, ourselves, and our loved ones from external threat against harm or violence.

The right to bear arms has served this country well. If we were to look at the pandemic of 2019, and while many have been sick and many have died from this disease, we have had a relatively peaceful and orderly response, especially in this country.

I do not think it is too hard to imagine a scenario where chaos and lawlessness prevailed on American streets and was the headline of the day. In fact, coinciding with the writing of this book, was the recent death of George Floyd which has brought about social unrest, upheaval, riots, and lawlessness to our city streets. Not to mention outrages calls to defund the police.

The national news covered one couple who stood guard outside their home, fully armed. Guess what happened, the rioters moved on and did not vandalize their property, without firing a shot. Unfortunately, you cannot say that about other parts of the city! Who will protect you now? The police agencies and law enforcement could be quickly and easily overwhelmed. If communications got knocked out, no one would be able to call law enforcement.

One thing most Bible believers understand relatively quickly when reading the Bible is the fact that evil does exist in this world. Evil can be found in the highest levels/places on Earth, even to the lowest places on Earth. And any prudent man or woman would be wise to take precautionary measures to protect against that evil.

For example, today, most of us lock our doors at night, most keep their vehicles locked as well, we keep valuables in safe places. You see, it is just a matter of good sense for those who want to take reasonable measures to protect themselves.

Liberal politicians would very much like to take this, I believe, God given and Constitutional right from the American people. The very Constitution that they are sworn to uphold, they seek to diminish or replace with a One World Constitution written by unbelievers and enforced by oppressive tyrannical rule.

The Bible and book of Proverbs teach us to avoid anger, to deescalate violence, to practice peace with all men. At times, men are called to lay down their life for the Lord, even turn the other cheek! Yet, Ecclesiastes 3 says: **"To everything there is a season, a time to every purpose under heaven."** Verse 3 says: **"a time to kill, a time to heal."** Also Verse 8 says: **"a time of war and a time of peace."** It is wise and prudent to get the whole counsel of God on this subject.

Though it is illegal in many states to carry an open or concealed firearm, many states require a special permit. Every state allows law abiding citizens to own, keep, and bear arms to protect life and property with varying interpretations of the law. I, as a Christian man, feel it is not only my right, but my duty, to the best of my ability, protect my home and family from any or all threats of harm.

The issue of gun control is "really about" disarming law-abiding citizens. I would argue, because of efforts in effect today by some attempting to breakdown our "time proven" moral ethics in our society, that the world is even a more dangerous place then years ago when the Second Amendment was adopted.

Again, gun control falls under the banner of World Government, a vote for gun control is a vote for worldwide control and tyranny. Their first step is always to disarm its citizens. Those in favor of gun control legislation are the first ones to build expensive, elaborate fences, home security systems, and armed guard details for their own safety, oftentimes paid for with taxpayers' money. We need to vote these hypocrites out of office for they are unfit for civil service.

The Bible says in Romans 13:4 (GW) version: **"The government is God's servant working for your good. But if you do what is wrong, you should be afraid. The government has the right to carry out the death sentence. It is God's servant, an avenger to execute God's anger on anyone who does what is wrong."** Another version that is the (CEB) Bible uses the wording: ...**"be afraid because it doesn't have weapons to enforce the law for nothing."**

So, I see God making provisions for mankind to both come under protection and come under punishment for disobeying the law. God does not have a problem with executing justice. So, I believe as Christians, we are to allow the authorities to administer the law on behalf of its citizens. Therefore, we should never take the law into our own hands.

Having said that there are times when using a firearm for personal protection is absolutely "acceptable." For God made provision, yet there will always be circumstances when the government is unable to intervene. That is when you should adhere to your particular "State laws" on the use of deadly force. Didn't we just read in scripture about, **"the right to carry out the death sentence."** Let me tell you brother, when someone breaks into your house, intent on doing your family bodily harm, that is NOT the time to "turn the other cheek."

The Bible says, in Mathew 5:39 (CEB) version: **"But I say to you that you must not oppose those who want to hurt you. If people slap you on your right cheek, you must turn the left cheek to them as well."** I believe this is a great translation of the scripture to illustrate the meaning. So, if someone wants to pick a fight with you, absolutely do not get physical with that person. Especially when you may only suffer some harm, such as a slap in the face, this will not justify violence in the eyes of the Lord. In fact, you might even win that person to the Lord through your display of self-control, gentleness, or love.

HOWEVER!!! if you are about to suffer some serious bodily injury, or even possible death of yourself, or if you are compelled to help another and as a last resort and final option, go for it! And give them everything you got!

There is one final thought on this subject which I hope will clear up any misunderstanding. There is one exception, that would be in the case of "martyrdom." A martyr is someone who sacrifices his "life for his faith." For example, a Christian might be faced with the dilemma of choosing whether they should or should not remain steadfast in their faith, even when confronted with a "death sentence" for doing so. That is a completely different scenario from what I've been discussing previously in this chapter. The Bible certainly talks about martyrdom and it is indeed a very real and sobering reality as well.

Matthew 28:20: "...lo, I am with you always, even unto the end of the world."

CLIMATE CHANGE

To a degree, climate change may indeed be real. In fact, the Bible predicted centuries in advance that increasingly large-scale destructive weather events would act as a "sign to the end of the world." However, it is not the same understanding to which the radical environmentalist movement believes or adheres.

According to scripture, God will punish those that destroy the earth. Although, I believe this may be a reference to nuclear weapons, God goes on to say in Revelations 11:18: "**He will destroy them which destroy the Earth.**" Also, God has a purpose for the Earth. Isaiah 45:18: "**God himself that formed the Earth and made it, he hath established it, he created it not in vain, he formed it to be inhabited.**" So, concerning climate change- what are the causes? What are the solutions? These should be questions which must be viewed in the <u>light of scripture.</u>

The Bible says that after Adam fell in Genesis by disobeying God's command, that God placed a "curse" upon the Earth. In Genesis 3:17 God says: **"cursed is the ground for thy sake- in sorrow shall though eat of it all the days of thy life."** That curse is still in effect today. We are all familiar with invasive insects, blight and seasonal droughts, also flooding, winds, hail, and similar "scourges" on our planet. These are just examples of damages that can be caused by what we understand as naturally occurring events.

Without God's perspective, we can easily become unbalanced and focused too much on the wrong issues and put unnecessary emphasis on our misguided business and not God's business! For God said in Isaiah 65:17: **"for behold, I create new heavens and a new earth."** So, you see, God has already made a provision found in His Word and gives us His answer to this sin ravaged Earth. He did not say, "And man will create a new planet."

Concerning climate, God has also revealed that there is coming a time when the ability, or lack of ability, to recognize our familiar weather patterns would indeed change. These would be a sign of fulfillment of end-time prophetic scripture. In Matthew 16:2, Jesus said: **"when it is evening, ye say, it will be fair weather, for the sky is red. And in the morning, it will be foul weather today, for the sky is red and lowering. O ye hypocrites, ye can discern the pace of the sky, but can ye not discern the signs of the times?"**

In other words, you have become familiar with common everyday weather patterns when these patterns no longer are common and predictable That is when these uncommon weather events must become an end-time sign unto you! So, increasingly destructive weather events are just one of multiple signs converging together in these last days. I believe that what is needed here is the correct response to the "yes" very real issue.

The Bible predicted these catastrophic events would occur in the last days and they would increase in both number and intensity. The first response should be to acknowledge the scriptural forecast. These events, therefore, they shall indeed occur, and we cannot stop them. They will occur worldwide, and they are one part of many sorrows that will afflict the Earth in the last days- Matt 24:7: **"and there shall be famines and pestilence and earthquakes, in diverse places."** Secondly, mankind's ability is extremely limited in scope to stop these events from afflicting the Earth.

In part, some of these weather events will come to grab our attention, others come to judge or even punish as well. Severe and even supernatural weather-related disasters are sometime results of the wrath of Almighty God against unrepentant sinners. (see the book of Revelation, chapters 8, 11, and 16) I have not found scripture to support the radical agenda to sound the "alarm" and make drastic wide-ranging efforts to alleviate mankind's "footprint" on the environment.

It would be unwise to credit "global warming" as the foremost cause which mankind should unilaterally work on, focus, and get behind to solve. Man's sinful, prideful, and vain attempts to save the planet, which apart from God would always elude him. You are putting the creation of God before the CREATOR. That is the same planet that God created originally, who permitted and allowed to become polluted.

We did not catch God "off-guard." He is not shocked or surprised, nor has He delegated to man the responsibility to return the Earth to its former glory prior to the industrial revolution. He is not sending man to hell because he drives a V8 instead of a Tesla or Prius.

If you are a radical environmentalist, your right standing with God should become your priority, then and only then will you allow God to be God and put His creation into His capable Hands- trusting God to recreate or restore the Earth on HIS timetable.

He alone has sovereign control over the Earth, He has some- times been known to use even the <u>forces of nature</u> themselves, in His dealings with mankind for both good and evil. Even bringing about a worldwide flood, in dealing with the wickedness of man. Most people are aware of the Biblical story of the great flood as told in the book of Genesis chapters 6-8 this is when the entire Earth was destroyed as we know it.

So, mankind's disobedience to God can be the cause of destructive weather events. The flood is not the only example we have in the Bible, but it is probably the most well-known. So, God preserved mankind's lineage by delivering only eight righ- teous people from the destruction of the great flood. They were Noah, (who walked with God) his son's and their wives. They were the only ones considered righteous in Gods eyes. So, God pronounced judgment on wicked sinners.

Today, once again, the Earth suffers from the results of man- kinds "inventions" or "science and technology." Our inventions and what we do with them are a result of "The Tree of Knowledge of Good and Evil" which Adam was told not to eat from, see Genesis chapter 2-3. Yet we know he did eat from it and we are still living with the consequences. Yet the Earth suffers (environmental dam- ages) for doing so.

Particularly, since the industrial revolution and man's growing technology, some of which can save lives, some can turn lights on, while still others are capable of destroying everything on the planet. Again, a mixture of (good and evil) Just another result and consequence of man's sin and rebellion against God. This all started way back in beginning in the Garden of Eden. It has never been God's plan for us to fix that on our own, even if we could, we cannot go back and change things, although again- this did not catch God off-guard- He knows the end from the beginning (Isaiah 46:10)- He had a plan, still has a plan, and we can trust Him. We can know that plan for ourselves; Jeremiah 29:11 says: **"For I know the plans I have for you"**- declared the Lord, **"plans to prosper you and not to harm you, plans to give you hope and a future."**

Without an all Powerful, Almighty, Supernatural God of the Bible, both Creator and Savior, I could see the need for mankind to come together and rescue the planet before we all become extinct. I mean, I do not want my offspring to inherit a post apocalypse, uninhabitable wasteland (as often portrayed by Hollywood.)

Obviously, we have done damage to the Earth, our air, and water. Yet, the Earth is indeed still "inhabitable." Don't worry- God is still in control. However, mankind's severe response and noble task to save the planet before it's too late is not what is on God's mind or agenda- not at all! I do not think we should ignore the issue, but neither should we panic- with a good measured response, deal with the issue responsibly, knowing we can survive on this planet for as long as it takes.

Eventually, God will bring an end to the question of mankind's sin, our salvation, and the restoration of all things. So, what is wrong with that? That should be common sense, right? However, with many that is just not the case.

The real danger of climate change is that it will be used as a catalyst to deceive and control the masses. It is important to know what the United Nations believes on this subject. A quote from their website is quite revealing: *"CLIMATE CHANGE IS THE DEFINING ISSUE OF OUR TIME. And we are at a defining moment, from shifting weather patterns that threaten food production, to rising sea levels that increase the risk of catastrophic flooding- the impacts of climate change are global in scope and unprecedented in scale, WITHOUT DRASTIC ACTION TODAY, adapting to these impacts in the future will be more difficult and costly."*

So, the U.N. claims climate change is the "defining issue of our time." Allow me to interject! Climate change is NOT the defining issue of our time. It is rather climate change "hysteria"; that is and will become a defining moment. People from all walks of life are sold out on climate change hysteria.

Again, our young ones are being indoctrinated on a level as never before. The U.N. is the defining global voice on this hysteria. This movement will become a cry for global governance and the micro-management of the Earth's resources. This can only lead to bondage and manipulation and may become a major issue "on the horizon" in are not-so-distant future.

There is more, the U.N. mandate continues, the *"human fin-gerprint"* on greenhouse gases- *"as populations, economies, and standards of living grow, so does the cumulative level of green-house gas (GHGS) emissions."* This sounds like a call for global poverty and population reduction.

Of course, these rules only apply to the masses, not the elites. I am sure they will have some kind of "buy in number," (millions of dollars) for exclusion rights, for those who can afford it. Sounds a bit sinister, maybe even vile! Finally, the U.N. Panel on Climate Change (IPCC) reports, it is categorical in conclusion: *"climate change is real and human activities are the main cause."* For them to take effective action *"would require rapid, far-reaching, and unprecedented changes in all aspects of society."*

Do you trust the U.N. liberals and other global elites to decide what far-reaching and unprecedented changes are necessary to combat epic-dangers of climate change? Potentially affecting all aspects of you and your families lives and futures. All for their VAIN ATTEMPT at dictating, controlling, and enforcing mankind's global impact and other business on the Earth?! Will you join in with the false panic and hysteria, and the "sky is falling" mentality?

Most of the planet's pollution is created by decisions and acts made by super wealthy elite owners and operators of large corporations, more so than by the hands of middle class or poorer people, who have no say in their decision making. However, they want us the common people to take the blame. Greed, bottom line profit margins, etc. usually drive and fuel these poor decisions.

However, God is far more concerned with YOU and ME and where we spend eternity. Yes, our right standing with God (which only comes through faith alone in God's mediator between He and man that is Jesus Christ.) Yes, when we allow God to work in us, changing us on the inside, dealing with sin in our lives, we come into right relationship with Him. He and He alone will once again recreate this planet Earth as is was in the Garden of Eden, and for man to inhabit with God and not apart from him with no more sufferings of sin and death.

One day soon, but not before man's coming failed attempt at world government, Christ shall establish His kingdom on the Earth, yet it will differ from what we know today. Isaiah 11:6-9 says: **"The wolf also shall dwell with the lamb, and the leopard shall lie down with the kid; and the young calf and the young lion and the fatling together, and a little child shall lead them. And the cow and the bear shall feed; their young ones shall lie down together, and the lion shall eat straw like the ox..."**

I want to comment on something said earlier about severe weather increasing in the last years and that is that Christians do not have to be in fear about that. We have been given the Word of God with scripture promises of protection that we can, by faith, speak and pray and learn to use effectively against all danger or perilous times. There have been many testimonies, even of hurricanes destroying entire blocks but leaving the believers' property untouched, themselves unharmed.

These kind of stories and miracles in the lives of true believers are common and do happen regularly. The truth is when a true believer does die, they do not die without hope. Neither do they die in fear of retribution or eternal punishment, but they enter a better world, and a better existence, an end to worldly suffering and physical pain.

Repent today if you are still unsaved or if you are a backslidden Christian. Please, do not put it off for another second. Put your trust in God, He will never disappoint you. You will be a new creation, no matter what you have done or what you have believed. He is a good God and if there is breath in your body, it is not too late.

II Corinthians 5:17 says: **"Therefore if any man be in Christ, he is a new creature: old things are passed away; behold, all things are become new."** You have nothing to lose but EVERYTHING to gain.

Revelation 12:7: "... And there was war in heaven."

MILITARY SPENDING

You know! War did not start on the earth. No, not at all. The truth is the Bible teaches that war began in "heaven", and even before "time" as we know it. Some liberal thinkers see war "generically" as such an immoral act that we must somehow, someday rise above. Maybe "universal peace" could be a "lofty" goal for mankind to attain to.

What is wrong with that? Certainly, the United Nations believes so. Well, once again, liberals make judgments outside of the realm of Biblical knowledge, and simply fail to acknowledge our fallen and imperfect nature, which at present will never allow us on our own and apart from God to realize any lasting , legitimate, or "universal" peace.

What about nuclear weapons? That can be a scary, sobering reality. What about foreign policy? Liberals just seem to never get it "right." We are living in a day where if we are ignorant of the times, if we lack proper discernment, if we don't have good judgment, if our leaders get inaccurate, misleading, and even false intelligence, even unwise guidance or counsel- we are heading for big trouble!

I am reminded of a very prophetic 1998 front page newspaper headline. The photographers snapshot captured then President Bill Clintons, historical visit to mainland China, including his visit to the excavation site and museum of China's "Terracotta Warriors" (an archeological find from the Qin Dynasty). In the photo Clinton could be seen extending his hand to shake the hand of a life size Chinese Terracotta soldier.

I am sure it was just a light-hearted gesture however the photo prophetically spoke volumes! This was a time our history when we began to export super computers and advanced satellite technology to China while we were in turn importing cheap plastic wares and children's toys. This was not a wise decision! Today, instead of being grateful to the U.S. for assisting there rise to super- power status, rather, we have been the recipient of threats and intimidation, by a formidable Chinese military machine, built in part with stolen American technology, and unwise trade agreements!

As Solomon wrote in Ecclesiastes 3:8: **"There a time for peace and there's a time for war."** Well thank GOD, we're in a time of relative peace in this country. But the wrong politician, the wrong Commander and Chief could easily, mistakenly, use this time of peace to let down our guard. They would not hesitate to defund the military and misuse the funding for some other wasteful project. To some politicians, the military is usually the first to get cut. I am telling you that NOW is the time to fund the military as never before! We must have a strong military as a deterrent in the times we're living in.

Some people and politicians alike live with a false sense of security and are blind to the very real threats in this world. It is like they are right there in front of them, yet they cannot recognize or acknowledge them. There are many leaders, some Evil Dictators, and a lot of Nations on earth today that would love to take America down and destroy her influence in the world.

America, with all her problems, is a beacon of light in this dark and potentially dangerous world we live in. Again, what does the Bible say? The Bible talks about the coming of a great time of war when peace will be taken from the Earth.

There will be a GREAT SWORD unleashed on the Earth. Revelation 6:4: says, ..."**and power was given unto him that sat thereon to take peace from the earth, and that they should kill one another: and there was given unto him a great sword.**" There are scriptures that describe in greater detail the wars that will come to pass, some describe the nations who are involved, others describe the devasting effects of modern weapons of mass destruction.

I have somehow known prophetically and with the knowledge of the scripture, and with the awareness of events in the news, that the "major" powers that be in the world have been both secretly and even openly (for decades now) building their militaries.

Not only are they stock-piling weapons, but they are aggressively developing and testing deadly new technologies for warfare. Even while at home, our own liberal politicians, routinely ignorantly with "full steam ahead" continue to make cuts and divert funding of our own military. That is completely oblivious to the ever growing and dangerous reality of the true condition of our current "collective" world.

We should never be ignorant of the fact that there are nations and leaders of the world who will one day be willing to initiate and prevail in what their minds would be a successful full-scale "nuclear" holocaust with the United States. Thank God not all of them are strategically poised to do so. Many such nations have either deliberately, or intuitively been preparing for the fulfillment of Revelation chapter 6:4 (to take peace from the earth)

In the U.S.A., some political parties are known to make cuts and others are known to build. By the end of the last Administration much of our military stockpile of conventional weapons had been depleted due to costly longstanding conflicts in the Middle East, not to mention our flatline economic conditions. Military cuts are the last thing we need in these times and would be highly irresponsible of any politician who is called to protect and defend, not only the Constitution but the American people, including strategic allies.

According to the Bible and according to reality, there is evil in the world, evil exists, we cannot ignore it like it will somehow go away. We should not pretend it will never threaten our nation and our American way of life. This is a dangerous proposition.

You cannot appease a tyrant who desires world domination, as was the case for Hitler and others, for some indeed tried. They only understand one thing and that is a power and/or forces greater than themselves. The Nazis and the Japanese had to forcibly be prevented from continuing to make war. Their war machine, their ability to make war, had to overwhelmingly be brought to a decisive end- that took military power, determination, guts, successful strategic operations, and countless lives. Also, don't forget the Grace of Almighty God.

That is a lesson learned in the not so distant past. Why does that continue to elude the minds of intellectuals, politicians, and everyone else that would try to disarm our vital military?

When Jesus returns, He will come in the sky and every eye shall see Him (Rev 1:7.) He warned about false Christs and false prophets doing great signs and wonders (Matt 24:24.) His return to set up His earthly kingdom and rule will not occur until nearly the end of the very last war, which I believe will occur in our own generation.

So be forewarned about a man that will "come in his own name" the Bible says John 5:43. He will come to rule the world and will succeed on some level, yet it will end in utter chaos and destruction. Who knows when some evil- minded leader will one day initiate a "global" war! It just takes one wrong leader, or one wrong event to ignite a "powder-keg" of destruction.

The Bible talks of a coming time of "trouble" unparalleled in history. Mathew 24:21: says, **"For then shall be great tribulation, such as was not since the beginning of the world to this time, no, nor ever shall be."** I tell you if you do not know God, don't put it off another day- give your life to JESUS CHRIST TODAY; knowing that whatever happens, He's got you!

7

Trump/Solomon

Overview of King Solomon

Solomon is reported to be the wisest man who ever lived, writing over three thousand Proverbs- including being accredited for writing at least three books of the Bible. These are the books of Proverbs, Ecclesiastes, and Song of Solomon. The book of Proverbs ranks among the many "favorite books" of the Old Testament being simple, easy to read, and informative.

It is packed full of wisdom and teaching on how to become a person of character, and how to become successful in every area of life.

King Solomon was the son of King David, whom God considered, a "man after His own heart" Solomon too knew this God of the Bible and was unashamed of seeking him. The Bible says, 1 Kings 3:3: **"Solomon loved the Lord, walking in the statues of David his father."** So, Solomon became King over Israel in place of his father David. Anyone can read the whole story if you would like to, in I Kings and 2 Chronicles in the Bible.

So, what Solomon did after becoming King was amazing. He made a thousand burnt offerings on the altar for God and the result of those offerings were that they got God's "attention." God said to Solomon (in a dream one night) in 1 Kings 3:5: **"ask what I shall give thee"**? Solomon replied, **"Give therefore thy servant an understanding heart to judge thy people, that I may discern both good and bad."** And the Bible says, **"and the speech pleased the Lord that Solomon had asked this thing."**

Then God said: **"Behold, I have done according to thy words; lo, I have given thee a wise and understanding heart."** The Lord was pleased with Solomon, that he asked this thing and did not ask for riches for himself, or the necks of his enemies.

The word "judge" when Solomon says, **"that I may judge thy people"** this can mean to *"govern"* or to *"litigate"* these *are* common terms still used in government today. So, in other words, Solomon asked God for the wisdom and good judgement to govern, litigate, and serve this great people whom God had placed under his dominion.

This was simply a humble acknowledgment and awareness of Solomon's very own weaknesses and human frailty. He was confessing his needful desire to walk in Godly wisdom, so that he might successfully accomplish his great calling in life. He sought out Godly counsel for the express purpose of governing the people.

I tell you, there has never been a time like today, when we needed Godly leadership. Also, Godly <u>wisdom</u> for our nation, our families, our children, and our households. DO NOT delay- Isaiah 55:6, **"Seek ye the LORD while He may be found."** Do not put it off. Many are depending on you!

I have found that there are numerous interesting and incredible parallels between the lives of King Solomon and Donald

Trump. King Solomon's works are recorded in the Book of I Kings and II Chronicles. I will approach these in two parts: First,

Part 1, Trump's personal and business life, and secondly,

Part 2, we will look at Trump's political life as President.

PART 1

Trumps Personal and Business life

Before we get into a breakdown of I Kings and II Chronicles scripture verses, I have made a few "general observations." God had a purpose and plan for both men. Both men were called to lead great nations. Solomon's desire was to have wisdom to lead his fellow Israelites after decades of war under his father David. Not unlike Trump, following decades of war in the Middle East under Bush and then Obama.

On a personal level, both men came from wealth. Trump was born into a successful upper-class businessman's household and certainly became accustomed to the finer things in life. Solomon was born into royalty, part of the King's household. When it comes to net-worth, both men exceeded that of their fathers.

Both men were well known, and you might say "famous." Solomon is still reputed as the wisest man in antiquity. Trump, a well-known American entrepreneur, went on to become a successful real estate developer and billionaire himself, both in the U.S. and abroad.

Each man married women from foreign countries. Solomon's first wife was the Egyptian daughter of Pharaoh. Trump's third marriage is to Melania from Slovenia, once a part of Yugoslavia. Also, his first wife, Ivana, was born in Czechoslovakia.

Both admired beautiful women. Trump was married three different times, including two former models, while Solomon had seven hundred wives.

Both men received help from their fathers. Trump reports that his father, Frederick, provided him with a million-dollar business loan, while Solomon's father, King David, made provisions for his construction of the "House of God." In 1 Chronicles 22 (NIV), in part, were **"a million talents of silver."**

Solomon took over the construction of the "House of God." Trump took over the family business, working and renaming it "The Trump Organization." In Chronicles 22:16- King David told Solomon to: **"arise and begin working."** Trump's older brother did not take over the family business, nor did Solomon's older brother take over the throne. Trump's elder brother died young and his life was wrought with trouble, while Amnon, King David's firstborn, died young and his life was also scandalized.

Solomon's father, King David, had deeply held religious beliefs and Frederick Trump was given the name Christ as his middle name, indicating his Christian family background. Solomon's earlier days were deeply devoted to God while in his latter days, he became somewhat of a "playboy"- I Kings 11:1: **"King Solomon loved many strange women."** A younger Trump once considered himself somewhat of a "playboy" or earned the reputation thereof and yet became deeply devoted to God in these latter years- meaning at this present time.

I Kings 5:3: "David, Solomon's father, was not permitted by God, to build an elaborate temple to God. **"he couldn't build a temple for the name of the Lord,"** that would have been in the City of Jerusalem, however Solomon was able." In a similar manner, Trump's father conducted business in lower to middle class Brooklyn and Queens. While his son Donald Trump eagerly set his sights on real estate in the more lucrative city of Manhattan. The pattern continues:

Trump made a living as a real estate developer, particularly in New York, including the infamous Trump Tower. Solomon is well known for his building programs as well including, "The House for the name of the Lord," or as it bears his name, "Solomon's

Temple." So, like Trump, Solomon was every bit of a successful real estate developer in his own time.

In fact, I Kings 6 (verses 2-10 and 15-22), even in the King James, reads like a set of "blueprints" including measurements and detailed descriptions. Moving on, we see it again in another part of the project with Verses 23-38 reading like a detailed "interior design" schedule.

In I Kings 7 (verses 2-12) again, we see more blueprints with interior design as well. In I Kings 6, there are descriptions of porches, windows of narrow lights, beams, doors and even a winding staircase. Solomon was not only busy constructing the "House of the Lord"- which was an elaborate perhaps "commercial real estate project"- but he also built the King's house, another elaborate residential construction. There was also the house of the "Forest of Lebanon" and separate home construction for his wife- Pharaoh's daughter.

In I Kings 7:5, it shows more doors and posts described as "square"- the same language used today for carpenters and builders- with windows specified as **"light was against light in three ranks"**- a nice touch. Verse 6 describes "porches and pillars."

The next parallel I would like to discuss, and it just gets better and better, is that Trump has never been your average real estate guy. His father focused on middle-class or poorer neighborhoods while Trump was the exact opposite. He ultimately ventured into the high dollar commercial office space, luxury condos, hotels, and upper-class residential properties. In fact, you can say Trump's brand is synonymous with luxurious living.

I quote the following from The Trump Organization's website: *"Trump, known as the Preeminent Developer of Luxury Real-Estate and is responsible for the finest portfolio of residential properties in the world, the Trump brand continues to elevate the global standard of luxury living,"* and then in 1 Chronicles

22:5, Likewise David tells his son, Solomon: **"and the house to be built for the Lord must be <u>exceeding magnificent</u>, famous, and glorious throughout all countries."**

One of the many responsibilities of a real estate developer, besides acquiring land and finalizing blueprints, would be to oversee the contracts, general labor, skilled tradesmen, superintendents, supervisors, human resources, the acquisition and purchasing of building materials, including steel, concrete, lumber, stone, etc. I Kings 5 reads the same as any modern construction project.

In verse 6, Solomon reaches out to Hiram, explaining his lumber supply needs along with the necessary labor and tradesmen. In verse 8 Hiram, after reviewing the contract and making sure he could fulfill the terms of the contract, says to Solomon, **"I consider the things which Thou sendest to me for. I will do all Thy desire concerning timber of cedar and concerning timber of fur."** Also, Hiram would be accountable for the transportation of materials to the agreed location. Verse 9: **"I will convey them by see in floats unto the place that thou should appoint me and will cause them to be discharged there."**

Solomon gave part payment to Harem in the form of agricultural goods based on a renewable yearly contract. In verse 18, Solomon, being the general contractor and the subcontractor, worked in cooperation with each other. In verse 12, Solomon realizing the size and scope of the project agreed to a limited partnership the two "made a league together."

In I Kings Verse 17: **"and the King commanded, and they brought great stones, costly stones and hewed stones, to lay the foundation of the house."** So, the overseer of labor began to supply the course building materials, similar to our version of concrete or stone building materials, they were finally ready to break-ground.

Once they began to build the House of the Lord, with blue-prints in hand, the Bible goes on to describe some of the great decadence involved in the construction. Besides the foundation stones, there is a reference to costly stones or what is commonly known today as limestone, granite and even marble. Marble is certainly costly, even today, and commonly used in high-end construction. Marble varies greatly in color depending on the quarry.

So, verse 14: **"So Solomon built the house and finished it."** Up until verse 14 the Bible focuses on the main construction, then afterwards the focus is on the interior work. In today's Carpenter language, this interior detail is called "finish" carpentry. The project certainly was not finished yet and here I come to my next point in verse 21: "**so Solomon overlaid the house within with pure gold in the construction.**"

The usage of gold is repeated 9 times in 18 verses, again it mentions costly stones that I have concluded as marble. When taken together, this use of costly marble and gold, even pure 24 karat gold- parallels the precise and well-known signature style of a famous real estate developer.

You guessed it- Donald Trump. He has a penthouse living space on the top three floors of Trump Towers located on 5th Avenue in NYC. You can easily find pictures on the internet. Truly, the most notable features right away would be the imported marble columns, 24 karat gold crown molding, embellishments, lamps and décor, and golden marble floors, walls, and carvings.

Even the Trump International Hotel in Las Vegas features 24 karat gold infused glass, with the Trump name at the top also in gold. Trump's private Boeing 747 jet features 24 karat gold plated ornaments and fixtures as well. So, I had thought the well-known (almost three foot tall) letters spelling "Trump Tower" in his Manhattan high-rise were covered in gold but I was mistaken. They are actually; constructed with polished brass. Then I found chapter 7, verse 25, which says: **"all these vessels which here are made to King Solomon for the House of the Lord were of bright brass."** You can't make this stuff up!

Additionally, I came across an older picture featuring a younger Trump on some job site adorned with a gold colored hardhat. For me, that just portrayed, symbolized, and embodies exactly the man I have been describing here. Do not think for a minute that Trump has been orchestrating his life around the writings of King Solomon; rather, God Almighty is the great orchestrator. Only He can know the end from the beginning.

In Solomon's own words, Ecclesiastes 1:9-10 says: **"the things that have been it is that which shall be and that which is done is that which shall be done and there is no new thing under the sun."** verse 10: **"Is there anything whereof it may be said, see, this is new"? it hath been already of old time, which was before us."**

The construction of the House of the Lord took seven years and the house for Solomon took thirteen years- this should be a testament to the skill and extravagance and extra fine details attributed to this building. Though done without the help of modern-day equipment, the workforce was numbered in thousands. Again, chapter 7 starts out as a construction plan for the house of the Forest of Lebanon.

Also, in verse 8, **"Solomon made also, a house for Pharaoh's daughter, whom he had taken to wife."** Do I need to say, Melania Trump has her own small private apartment on the 33rd floor of Trump Towers? That is in the <u>same</u> building where they share a penthouse suite. Verse 8: **"and his house where he (Solomon) dwelt had another court within the porch which was of the like work"** or similar design. This portion of scripture seems to connect the two, that is, Solomon's house, either connected or not far apart from Pharaoh's daughter's house.

Having said that, let me back up and go back to verse 7. **"Then he made a porch for the throne where he might judge…"** The throne is an official symbol and used by kings to rule and reign and conduct the affairs of the Kingdom, including Royal decrees and various judgments and business matters.

Trump tower is the official home of the Trump Organization's Corporate office and business headquarters. Here, Trump acted as Chairman, although he handed over his business to his sons while attending to his duties of the Office of the President.

As we discuss thrones, there is another interesting fact, in chapter 10 and verse 18-19: **"Moreover the king made a great throne of ivory and overlaid it with the best gold. The throne had six steps…"** Just as before, I related Solomon's throne with conducting the king's business; the Trump Tower also being a place for Trump's business. The throne had **"six steps,"** while the unique architecture of Trump Tower contains an unusual six steps facade, which can be seen from 5th Avenue.

Now, we shift from looking at Trump and Solomon as real estate moguls to the day-to-day duties of Legislating and Commerce and the "peoples" business.

1 Kings 10:20, ..."upon the six steps:
there was not the like made in any kingdom"

PART 2

Trumps political life

Even before Trump was inaugurated on January 20, 2017, the once nosedived sluggish economy, began to make record upturns. It was almost as if God was showing his "divine favor." This of course, in part, was in anticipation of the fresh, positive, and confident outlook of the coming President.

In a similar fashion, Solomon also upon coming into power, sought ambitious building projects to include an elaborate home for himself, including the infamous "Temple" for the Lord. This too was a fresh, and confident showing of Gods divine favor and blessing. These ambitious projects required strong economic conditions to fund the vast amounts of costly building materials and enormous labor force.

Another similarity between both men is, they each had significant skills regarding "trade agreements." Solomon established trade throughout the world. The kings' ships would regularly bring imports of, **"gold and silver, ivory, apes, and peacocks,"** I Kings chapter 10:22, and other forms of commerce. The nation enjoyed years of peace and prosperity.

Even though the nation was in a time of peace, Solomon built a formidable military including a strong Navy and Army comprised of men, chariots and horses. Trump also upon taking office, got to the business of rebuilding our military.

Solomon also met with leaders of many nations. The Bible says, 1 Kings 4:34, **"And there came of all people to hear the wisdom of Solomon."** So too, did Trump meet with foreign dignitaries as part of the business of the President.

Next, I Kings 8, verses 26-53: chronicles a powerful and anointed prayer and dedication ceremony upon the completion of the House of the Lord or Solomon's temple. Reading this lengthy prayer, I get a real sense of Solomon's intercession for the people. Verse 44: **"If the people go out to battle against the enemy..."** **"and shall pray unto the Lord."** verse 46: **"Hear thou in heaven their prayer in their supplication and maintain their cause."** This revelation goes deep. I mean, you need to see this with your spiritual eyes.

I do not know how many Christians realize the vicious attacks that our President Trump has been made to endure from the liberal and ruthless bloodthirsty media. These are direct attacks against the Church and Christians everywhere- including their values.

If you were to remove Trump, those same vicious assaults would be felt directly upon the Church Herself. So, whether you realize it or not, Trump is truly "standing in the gap." He is taking the brunt of the abuse targeted at us- the conservative Christians. When you read these few verses with that in mind, it tells a different story. Also, we the Church truly are, and have been, in a battle against the enemy. That is the ungodly and the liberal hatred against Trump, the Church, and Christian values.

I Kings 8:46: Solomon continues to intercede, **"if they sin against thee, (for there is no man that is not) and thou be angry with them, and deliver them to the enemy"** then verse 48: ...**"and so return unto thee with all their heart, and with all their soul."** And verse 49: **"then hear thou their prayer..."** **"and maintain their cause,"** verse 50: **"and forgive thy people that have sinned against thee."**

Just a man, a King for that matter, caring for his people. I see that very same heart and attitude in President Trump every time he talks about the American people. Not always when he is quarreling with his sworn enemies, but I see it from time to time and I do believe it comes from the heart. I also believe it is 100% genuine.

Let me ask you, do you see any liberals, politicians, leaders, etc. putting the righteous people ahead of themselves? I mean, Christians! I am not referring to lawless and violent criminal protesters or militant- LGBTQ, Trump haters, flag burners, and unprincipled people. I again refer to good, honest, law abiding and morally outstanding Christians and individuals.

Really, backing Trump, either by vote or by prayer, is synonymous with backing Christians and their values in society. Not because Trump is so great, or that he himself is some morally just, outstanding figure, or example. No, it is his "calling and his position" that is to be appreciated and respected.

Solomon was a good man, yet not a perfect one. He stood in the gap for the people, he was not without controversy, yet it was his position, title, and righteous deeds that were significant, powerful, and effective.

More importantly, his position and title were given to him by God's grace- neither was it earned through righteous deeds- it is the sovereign hand of God that was at play and that is why it is so important for people to realize. And why it is so important to get onboard with what God is doing for individual lives in America as well?

In like manner, Solomon foresees the people trespassing against God, and beginning in verse 31: **"if any man trespasses against thy neighbor or smitten down before the enemy, when heaven is shut up, and there is no rain, if there be in the land famine with each trespass,"** Solomon pleads with God, **"then hear thou in heaven."** (repeated overall 7 times) verse 8:54: **"and it was so, that when Solomon had made an end of praying all this prayer and supplication unto the Lord, he arose from before the alter of the Lord, from kneeling on his knees with his hands spread up to heaven,"** In this scene, I can see Trump's name being where Solomon's name was and I can see Trump kneeling, hands raised to God, as well.

Trump, no doubt, has been moved by the Christian prayer intercessors and influences in and around his life. He consistently stands behind Christian principles and acknowledges our Nation's rich Christian Judeo heritage.

Not being in his inner circle I cannot give first-hand accounts of his faith, but ultimately, only God knows a man's heart, so this is a good place to reveal one of several prophetic words given by Kim Clement on April the 4th 2007- *"There will be a praying President, not a religious one. I will fool the people says the Lord, hear the word of the Prophet to you. As a King, I will open that door that you prayed about, you will be elected. He will not be a praying President when he starts, but I will put him in office, then I will baptize him with the Holy Spirit in my power says the Lord of Hosts."*

Trump took a stand on December 6th, 2017 and we became the first nation to officially recognized "Jerusalem" as the Capital City of Israel. This declaration set in motion the process of relocating the United States Embassy, from Tel Aviv, to the ancient Biblical City of Jerusalem. On May 14th, 2018, a full seventy years after the birth of the Nation. Our new embassy officially opened in the ancient city. Trump came under fire from liberal leaders around the world, including the United Nations.

This was a move that strengthened our bond and commitment towards our Democratic allies of Israel and the Holy Land. Coincidentally, Jerusalem is also the former home of "Solomon Temple," and the place of Solomon's prayer of dedication, as we just discussed, in I Kings, chapter 8. Another unusual parallel!

I Kings 9:15: talks about a **"levy"** that Solomon raised. A levy according to the Google Dictionary means, *to "impose a tax, fee, or fine on"* usually paid to the government for various reasons and under various circumstances. The Dictionary.com definition, *"To impose (a tax) to levy a DUTY ON IMPORTS"*

Solomon begins at this point to connect the levy with, "economic-power" and well-being, including funding for building projects and expansion into certain cities, including the "Wall" of Jerusalem, chapter 9:15. **"And this is the reason of the levy which king Solomon raised."** Trump was opposed by the liberals to provide funding for the wall at our Southern border, yet Trump went on to begin building the wall without them. I Kings 9:19:

"Desired to build in Jerusalem and in Lebanon and in all the land of his dominion."

As Solomon began to focus more on verse 19, **"cities,"** he had entered more into the political realm and less of the "real estate developer" realm. **"in all the land"** Here he must have begun to rely more on his "chain of command" then his own ability to focus on each individual construction project, as he did in the beginning.

Though Trump favored New York City and Manhattan, he too ventured out to cities across America and foreign nations as well. In Trump and Solomon's "worlds," they each began to develop more toward a "political" position and operation then a business one. They would now predominately delegate to separate mid-level Governors and appointed leaders. In the same way, Trump began with the business of "real estate" and later in life, the business of "politics" Again Trump used to build buildings now he largely delegates his authority.

In the beginning of the verse, **"all the cities of the store that Solomon had, and the cities for his chariot, and the cities for his horsemen..."**- this verse sounds like good, favorable, and prosperous economic activity and conditions. Verse 19: **"all the cities"**- as in the U.S.A. and all the states too- had good, economic activity. Ultimately, it begins with the peoples' small businesses, government contracts, corporations and other trade and commerce. Taken together and with the right leadership and God's good blessings, these things can produce a thriving economy where all people benefit.

In I Kings 9:20 and 21, the verse describes Israel's foreign enemies whom Israel was **"not able to utterly destroy."** It says that Solomon **"levy a tribute of bond service..."** This levy was not a tax imposed on the children of Israel. Neither in Trump's situation has he raised the peoples' taxes, it was not on the American citizens, but on "foreign nations" not considered "friendly." Even nations that may have taken advantage America in the past. Yes, and (when it comes to America) I am talking about China! Although, Trump is finally holding them accountable, we have not "utterly destroyed them" as well.

Verse 22: **"But the children of Israel did Solomon make no bondmen."** This verse shows Solomon's heart and dedication for his people, as does Trump to the American people.

If it were not for the American people, I think Trump may have said "to hell with this job." He has enough to live comfortably for the rest of his life. It is his love of country and the patriotic citizens of the land that went to the polls which helps him to persevere to this very day.

I must say that verse 21 in some of the Bible translations, have used the term "slaves" or "forced labor." This may, in fact, be the case in ancient Israel. I cannot say with certainty, yet the terms used for "levy" and "tribute" are defined in the English language as tax or tariff.

Most Americans are aware of tariffs placed upon China by the Trump Administration. These overdue tariffs apply to imports of many manufactured goods, so in an indirect way, this could impact the average laborer or working-class factory workers in China and elsewhere, similarly to Solomon's "levy" on foreign workers.

Next, I Kings touches on King Solomon's military ambitions, verse 22: **"they were men of war, and his servants and his princes, and his captains and rulers of his Chariots and his horseman."** Here we have described military men, government officials, and military officers and army commanders of whom Trump's title as Commander in Chief fits well.

Verse 26: **"and King Solomon made a Navy of ships..."** Solomon, even in a time of peace, took advantage of a strong economy and was busy building the formidable military. Liberals never see a need for a strong military, perhaps they have forgotten the many lessons from history. However, Trump immediately acknowledged the need and promptly began to back, finance, and assist in restoring our fledgling military.

After long years of war in the Middle East, dwindling supplies and evolving threats around the globe, America indeed must have the greatest military on Earth- we are not warmongers, conquerors, or tyrants, but ambassadors of goodwill and peace brokers.

We do not have a perfect record, nobody does, yet more often than not, it is America that comes to the aid of oppressed people, rescue operations, foreign assistance, doctors and medicine, food, and most importantly- the gospel.

It is not the Communists or Socialists that stand for the rights of the people. Sadly, liberals cannot get their minds around that- they need a change of heart, hopefully that will happen.

In I Kings 10:1: **"when the Queen of Sheba heard of "the fame of Solomon" concerning the Name of the Lord, she came to prove him with hard questions."** Here we have two points- one being the fame of Solomon. Yes, Solomon was famous in ancient times and on some level, even today. Also, you could say even prior to politics, "the fame of Trump" mirrors that of Solomon. He was very well known in the business world and later in television with "The Apprentice." You might say, a "household name" here in America as well.

Point number two- **"the Queen came to prove him with hard QUESTIONS."** You know the scribes and pharisees did the same thing to Jesus. Matthew 22:35 is one example: **"then one of them, a lawyer, asked him a question tempting him..."** then in verse 46: **"Jesus, growing tired of them and in return, asked them a question of which they were unable to answer.."** then finally the verse says, **"no man, from that day forth asked him anymore questions."**

The reason I brought this up is, well, today they do the same thing to Trump! Who? The media. Myself being somewhat of a news junkie, I cannot count the number of times that dysfunctional liberal journalists deliberately shoot loaded questions at Trump, attempting to provoke some "less than Presidential" response.

Surely, they are hoping to catch him off guard or produce some "newsworthy" event or reaction, or just try to make him look like a fool, that is, if they could! Yet, these very same journalists treat liberals with white gloves and soft questions. Truly hypocritical, defiant behavior, and double standard, unfitting of their vocation, giving our "once respectable" news media organization in this country a bad name and worse reputation.

It was famed Nazi propaganda Joseph Goebbels who *said, "if you tell a lie big enough and keep repeating it, people will eventually come to believe it."* That is what the liberals are hoping for. He went on to say, *"the truth is the greatest enemy of the state."* Well, I certainly will go along with that statement. That's pretty much what I have been talking about all along. I hope that is not the condition of the "state" we live in. It is not the conservative political party "state." Is this the state you want to partner with? Is this the state you want for your children?

To continue on, I Kings 10:1, refers to **"the Queen of Sheba"**- she can be likened to a visiting foreign dignitary who may fall in the category of someone whom King Solomon's and President Trump's position, may formally meet with, and discuss official business. Frequently, the Presidents meet with foreign leaders both abroad and at home, and Trump is no exception.

In fact, Trump- in my assessment- has a great deal of finesse, respect, and dignity, as well as loyalty to his "World Leader" friends and a staunch outspoken opponent to his enemies.

That strikes a good balance in issues of foreign affairs with just enough humility to meet with leaders like North Korea's Kim Jong-un and enough sensibility to not put too much trust in leaders such as Vladimir Putin or Xi Jinping of China. He is graceful enough to extend his hand and discerning enough to not be gullible. This is one of Trump's strong points.

One final comparison in 1st Kings, we see a skillful Solomon functioning in the form of numerous foreign trade deals and negotiations- this parallel may be one of Trump's overall finest points. One of Trump's books, "The Art of the Deal" promotes an accumulation of his years of "hands on" experience, knowledge, and wisdom which serves the White House and the American people well.

Trump revisited unwise, outdated, and one-sided international agreements. We were losing billions of dollars of U.S. taxpayers' money that was being funneled into dark holes. Overturning years of senseless policies of careless bureaucrats. Trump began to hold these politicians accountable and renegotiate sensible commerce in favor of the American people.

So, we are certainly living in a time where God has been unmistakably revealing profound truths contained in the scriptures. This was not the case fifty years ago! Not on this level. I hope this book helps to get the peoples' attention. We are no doubt in a season of change! DO NOT ALLOW YOURSELF TO MISS OUT ON God's plan for your life!

8

Past Presidents

Introduction

How many modern-day leaders do you know who have publicly or privately called upon divine providence during their tenure? Amazingly, other than our presiding President, you would need to go back a while to really get a sense of leadership's reliance on divine providence.

There is the "once very-well known" story of how George Washington, Commander of the Continental Army, miraculously survived a most certain fate. This was, of course, none other than divine providence as the reason for his supernatural protection. (I cover this under G. Washington) You see, God had a special purpose for him, God watched over him, even in the worst of battles.

What most people don't know was that he was a man of prayer and faith in God, and of course would later become our first President of the United States. In a similar manner, God has continued to watch over this nation, even from our earliest inception. At a time when the founding fathers were drafting the

Declaration of Independence and the Constitution of the United States of America, again you can see by simply examining the documents themselves, we get a sense of the founding fathers' reliance and familiarity with the scriptures. Although they sometimes use words or phrases that we are not too familiar with today, you still just cannot fake it. You either walk with God or you do not.

A "one time" formality of putting your hand on the Bible and swearing an oath does not make you credible, consistent, or more importantly a profitable Christian. The Bible teaches that you will know people by their "fruit"- as a tree or other plant is also known by their fruit, see (Matthew 7: 16-20) If you claim to be Christian, there should be visible signs and consistent fruit. Also, you cannot always judge people based on their past, that is not always a good barometer. people can change, as I certainly did.

Though sometimes, it is just the little things- I know Washington publicly "kissed" the Bible on Inauguration Day as an act of affection and respect on public display. Another beloved President was Abraham Lincoln. Like Washington, Lincoln was considered one of our great Presidents. In more recent times, we have President Ronald Reagan who entered office by divine protocol as well.

Ecclesiastes 1:9: **"The thing that hath been, it is that which shall be, and that which is done is that which shall be done: and there is no new thing under the sun."** During the research of the history of our American presidents, I could not help but realize **"there is nothing new under the sun."**

There were good Democrats and bad Republicans and good Republicans and bad Democrats. Corruption in the government is nothing new. Also, honest men of good integrity were nothing new as well. Some past presidents had to choose between becoming a preacher or politician. Others were simply good businessmen.

Some started out poor while others came from wealth. Some were deeply religious some others were not. Some served in the military, others were lawyers, some were loved, and others hated.

I noticed Franklin D. Roosevelt's infamous "fireside chats"-as they were affectionately called. Roosevelt reached out to the people who elected him through their modern-day radio broadcasts. That reminded me of how President Trump reached out to his constituents via our modern internet technology of the day, and his "Twitter campaign," whereby he could bypass the corrupt unfavorable media.

Over the years, America has both prospered economically and struggled terribly, has been united as well as divided, war and peace, good times and bad, but have always managed to overcome and survive to "live and fight again." By the grace of God, hopefully we will continue to do so!

I do not think this book would be complete without including some interesting facts and quotes from a few of our former American Presidents.

Romans 4:17, "...I have made thee a father of many nations."

George Washington
1st President, from 1789 until 1797

Washington was considered the "Father of our Country." He became the Commander of our Continental Army. He fought in the Revolutionary War and was the General Overseer of the Constitutional Convention, where we get our United States Constitution.

Prior to the Presidency, a younger Washington fought in the French and Indian War. In a battle called Monongahela, there he miraculously survived a most certain fate. He writes- *''by the All-Powerful dispensations of Providence, I have been protected beyond all human probability or expectation. For I had four bullets through my coat, and two horses shot under me, yet I escaped unhurt, although death was leveling my companions on every side of me.''* I cannot help but to recall, Psalms 91:7: a popular and well known scripture for "protection"- **"A thousand shall fall at thy side, and ten thousand at thy right hand; but it shall not come nigh thee."**

Fifteen years after, in a chance encounter with the same Indian Chief who gave the order to take aim on Washington at Monongahela, admits *"twas all in vain, a power mightier far than we, shielded you."* The Chief, by some unction, proceeded to speak prophetically over Washington: *"there is something bids me speak in the voice of prophecy. Listen! The Great Spirit protects that man and guides his destinies- he will become the Chief of Nations, and a people yet unborn will hail him as the founder of a mighty empire. I am come to pay homage to the man who is the "particular favorite" of heaven, and who can never die in battle."* This wonderful story about George Washington was once taught in our schools. What a shame today, that our children do not know this!

Isaiah 55:4, "Behold, I have given him for a witness to the people, a leader and commander to the people."

Abraham Lincoln

16th President, from 1861 until 1865

Lincoln came into office during troubling times. The nation was being divided between North and South. He worked hard and was willing to fight to abolish slavery. The Civil War began just over a month after his election and would not come to an end until mere days before his assassination. Having said that, I just can't shake the fact that Lincoln was called for "such a time as this" as was Esther in the Bible: see (Esther 4:14).

Also, he left us with many great words of wisdom. Including the following: *"those who deny freedom to others, deserve it not for themselves"* and *"Under a just God, cannot long retain it."*

Quick note! During my research, you know I came across some so called "Historians" claiming Lincoln was an atheist. These outrages claims can be detrimental to those who don't know any better, especially with the freedom of information on the internet. The devil wants to erase our Christian heritage all together. Today, it is our responsibility to pass the truth along to our children, we cannot any longer depend on the government.

Tell me what you think after the following quote from Lincoln on the Bible. *"In regard for this great book, I have this to say; It is the best gift God has given to man. All the good Savior gave to the world was communicated through this great book."* Also he said these words, *"I can see how it might be possible for a man to look down upon the earth and be an atheist, but I cannot conceive how a man could look up into heaven and say there is no God."* Great wisdom from a great man! Psalm 14:1, says: **"The fool hath said in his heart, there is no God."**

These words should be preserved in our history books. Our children should be well acquainted with our rich Christian heritage! Lincoln went on to warn future generations, *"America will never be destroyed from the outside, if we falter and lose our freedoms, it will be because we destroyed ourselves."*

In April of 1863, Lincoln, along with the Senate, designated our first official National Day of Prayer and Humiliation. The proclamation contains numerous references and acknowledgement to Almighty God, his relationship to our Nation, and man's need for repentance. It is available on the internet if you want to check it out. Surprisingly, his words are ever so prophetical today.

"We have forgotten the gracious hand which preserved us in peace, and multiplied and enriched and strengthened us; and we have vainly imagined, in the deceitfulness of our hearts, that all these blessings were produced by some superior wisdom and virtue of our own. Intoxicated with unbroken success, we have become too self-sufficient to feel the necessity of redeeming and preserving grace, too proud to pray to the God that made us!" I want to tell you, we all need to repent in this country, we are all sinful men (and women) regardless of politics, however, this is a perfect description of the ungodly liberals in this country!

First, they have "forgotten God" that made this great nation. It is by their own superior wisdom, secular virtues, and immoral values that gives them the right to govern. Without God, the intoxication with "unbroken success" so poetically captured by Lincoln, is a perfect picture of the unspoken reality that liberals subconsciously somehow award themselves.

This distinction of perpetual success, only enforces their false confidence in their own carnal abilities, once again, the "ungodly" are "too proud to pray to the God that made us." Lincoln, in a very brief review of some of his own quotes, describes a man of great wisdom beyond his years and rich faith towards God, without an atheist bone in his body.

Isaiah 22:1: "...and I will commit thy government into his hand."

Ronald Reagan
40th President 1981-1989

Reagan started out as a Hollywood Liberal. However, times changed and so did his beliefs and he was elected Republican Governor of California in 1967. Reagan was always a fierce opponent of Communism. He was accredited to winning the Cold War with former Soviet Union. He was extremely popular with the people and known as the great communicator, he also had a solid faith in God and interest in Bible prophecy.

Most don't realize he fought hard, yet without success, to reinstate prayer in the public schools- even proposing a constitutional amendment. Certainly, he had his heart in the right place, yet unfortunately he was unable to rally enough support for the amendment.

Going back some years to one Sunday in October of 1970, still while Governor of California, a small group gathered at

Reagan's home in Sacramento, California. In a "somewhat awkward" moment of prayer, The Holy Spirit came upon Mr. George Otis and he began to speak prophetically saying; *"If you (Reagan) walk uprightly before Me, you will reside at 1600 Pennsylvania Avenue."* This was a full ten years before his Presidential election. And so, God revealed his calling on President Reagan that day.

A similar event took place in the life of Solomon, recorded in I Kings 9:4-5 when God said: **"If thou wilt walk before me, as David thy Father walked, in integrity of heart, and in uprightness, to do according to all that I have commanded thee, and will keep my statutes and my judgements, then I will establish the throne of thy kingdom upon Israel forever."**

So, Reagan was not merely elected President, he was also uniquely called by God and "chosen." Within weeks of Reagan taking office, on March 30, 1981, while leaving a conference at the Washington Hotel, Reagan was nearly assassinated when shot in the chest, the bullet just missing his heart but piercing his lung. After two hours in surgery, Reagan made a full recovery.

Reagan's survival from the failed assassination attempt, to some, would come to be recognized as the "Breaking of the Tecumseh Curse" or the 20 year Presidential curse, being 140 years old (which I will cover at the end of this chapter.)

Leviticus 26:15: "And if you despise my statutes, or if your soul abhor my judgements, so that ye will not do all my commandments, but that ye break my covenant"...

Barack Obama
44th President, 2009-2017

When Obama first hit the stage, he was viewed as somewhat of a rock star, or "Messiah" like figure, among Democratic circles and media. Winning a Nobel Peace Prize (apparently for unknown reasons) just nine months into his first term. He presided eight years over what was called "the Great Recession." Gas prices soared exceeded $4.00 a gallon (an all-time high) and he was unable to break the country free from its economic woes.

Obama famously lit up the White House in rainbow colors in celebration of the Supreme Court decision legalizing same sex marriage in June of 2015. In 2011, he repealed Clinton's "Don't

Ask, Don't Tell" policy and allowed for gays to openly serve in the military, along with 2009 Hate Crimes Prevention Act. He also supported a ban on "conversion therapy" which in fact does contain some barbaric forms of behavior modifications. However, the ban also included prayer and Christian counseling- which for some, had produced miraculous results.

In 2013, Obama became the first President to speak at a national Planned Parenthood Conference. In his speech, he says *"After decades of progress, there's still those who want to turn back the clock to policies more suited to the 1950's than the 21st century."* This is sad when progress is doing away with God given restraints, statues, and commandments, which are for our own good and protection.

Although the 1950's were difficult times concerning civil rights, the American public at large made room for God in their daily lives. Families attended church regularly, a time when it was legal to pray in our schools and universities, a time when women waited until marriage, honoring their virginity, a time when Hollywood budgeted 13 million dollars (in 1956) for their blockbuster "The Ten Commandments," a time when America was emerging as the great world superpower, and yes, abortion varied by state but was illegal under most circumstances. Today, it's a second thought. I think if we keep "making progress" as liberals would eventually like, eventually you will bump heads with the devil himself. Obama's speech ends with *"Thank you Planned Parenthood. God Bless you. God Bless America. Thank you."* I'm not sure that God blessed Planned Parenthood, sounds misguided to me.

Obama revoked George W. Bush's Executive Order # 13435 on June 20, 2007 entitled *"EXPANDING APPROVED STEM CELL LINES IN ETHICALLY RESPONSIBLE WAYS."* Bush's order called for *"Stem cells derived by ethically responsible techniques"* and *"without violating human dignity or demeaning human life..."* The Order further states *"The destruction of NASCENT (beginning to exist) life for research violates the principles that no life should be used as a mere means for achieving the medical benefit of another. Human embryos and fetuses, as living members of human species ARE NOT RAW MATERIALS to be exploited or commodities to be bought and sold. The Federal Government has a duty to exercise responsible stewardship of taxpayer funds, both supporting medical research and respecting ethical and moral boundaries."*

Evidently, these moral restrictions proved too much for Obama, his Executive Order # 13505 of March 9, 2009 entitled *"REMOVING BARRIERS TO RESPONSIBLE SCIENTIFIC RESEARCH INVOLVING HUMAN STELL CELLS"* to fund and conduct human embryonic stem cell research has been LIMITED by Presidential actions. The purpose of this Order is to REMOVE THESE LIMITATIONS. Finally, *"to enhance the contribution of America's scientists to important new discoveries and new therapies for the BENEFIT OF MANKIND."*

The sad truth is the results of embryonic stem cell research can be best described as "How to Play God" more than their promise of any real or practical medical breakthroughs or cures to mankind's age old diseases and afflictions, which as of today, remain at a constant zero.

They hungerly eat up our tax dollars while they are learning how to implant human stem cells into animal embryos and other bizarre forms of "research" which is great if you enjoy horrific science experiments. Yes, it is once again the age old, sinful, fallen man syndrome- rejecting God and forging a bright new path of utter darkness and depravity which is still looming on the horizon; and funded with our tax dollars- a sickening legacy.

For science is their god and their god demand's human sacrifice and a fresh supply of innocent blood. How will that turn out for good? I thank God it wasn't my signature or "stamp of approval" on Executive Order 13505- how about you? I think the Apostle Paul did well in describing this contradiction in Romans 3:8: **"Let us do evil that good may come."**

Decisions often have consequences. Obama's record support for Planned Parenthood, including his removal of "limitations" on embryonic stem-cell research, formed the "Perfect Storm" when shocking revelations of Dr. Mary Gatter (Planned Parenthood Executive) came to light as she "lightheartedly" remarked of her desire for an expensive Lamborghini sports car based on revenues of proceeds of the sale of the aborted fetuses in various stages of development. These included "body parts" which also may require "modified" abortion procedures to avoid crushing or destroying "tissues" for providing more valuable and desirable fetuses.

This undercover video was caught "live" to the horror of most Americans. In retrospect, a look backwards, we still have no fulfilled hope, cures, or groundbreaking promises for cancer, including miracle drugs, or treatments and I doubt the "good doctor" has her Lamborghini either.

Although Lincoln initiated the first National Day of Prayer in 1863, it was not 1952, ninety years later when President Harry Truman finally signed it into law. Additionally, many Presidents hosted the event with a, "simple Celebration" and "Prayer" at the White House.

In 2016, Obama broke from tradition and excluded the White House Ceremony, instead he issued this Proclamation *"Our Country was founded on the idea of religious freedom."* Obama acknowledges accurately our Freedom from State Controlled Religion. *"Every day, women and men use the wisdom gained from humble prayer to spread kindness and to make our world a better place. Faith communities at home and abroad have helped feed the hungry, heal the sick and protest innocents from violence, nurturing communities with love and understanding... one of our most sacred responsibilities is to give ourselves in service to others. The threats of poverty, violence and war around the world are all too real. Our faith and our earnest prayers can be cures for the fear we feel as we confront these realities."*

Although, I shouldn't knock anyone's effort to acknowledge religion, faith, and prayer, a careful reading of Obama's words can be very revealing. First, Obama does not quote or elude to one scripture verse. Secondly, Obama's words reveal the liberal view and beliefs about the Christian religion. You see, liberal elites see Christianity as perhaps a beneficial yet non-vital role in society. Ultra-liberal, Karl Marx, called it the "opiate" of the masses, in his mind the effect of "getting high" as a way for weak people to deal with day to day life.

Sure, it's good to "spread kindness, feed the hungry and to give ourselves in service," these are all fine qualities and upstanding moral values, yet this next part of Obama's proclamation spells it all out. Listen carefully. *"The threats of poverty, violence and war around the world are all too real."* I agree so far, *"our faith and our earnest prayers can be cures for the fear we feel as we confront these realities."*

So, to summarize or paraphrase, faith and prayer can help us with feeling afraid, as we confront these realities, that is, not with prayer or humility, seeking God for wisdom, as "Lord, how can I address the threats of poverty, violence and war?" What can I, as President, do to affect change? And how can I use the power and influence that comes with the office of the President and this great responsibility? Lord, help me, give me your wisdom, especially when I feel totally inadequate to address these problems.

Instead of, "cause me not to fear, as I go about confronting the business of the President." I tell you I do not think this is a sincere prayer, and likely will have little results. There is a subtle but profound difference. One sees religion as an occasional crutch, whereby I go about my business, and the other sees their faith in Christ as a foundation stone for EVERYTHING I do. One makes foolish decisions and unwise choices and the other walks in wisdom and the power of God, with the backing of heaven.

So, liberals "tolerate" Christianity as long as they're feeding the hungry or showing kindness or some form of charity, just stay in your place and don't get involved in politics. Stay out of the business of running the kingdom or the affairs of governance or any real impact on society.

But, most of all, do not give the call for the "American people" to: "*abstain on that day, from their ordinary secular pursuits, and to unite, at their several places of public worship and their respective homes, in keeping the day Holy to the Lord and devoted to the humble discharge of the religious duties proper to that solemn occasion*" as did Abraham Lincoln at the city of Washington, "*this thirtieth day of March in the YEAR OF OUR LORD One Thousand, Eight Hundred and Sixty-three.*"

Obama admitted he was a member of Rev. Jeremiah Wright's Trinity United Church of Christ for the last 20 years that was in 2008, including performing his and Michelle's wedding ceremony along with their daughters' baptisms. Obama had to distance himself from Wright after a controversial sermon appeared where Wright said, I quote, "*In defense of African-Americans, this government gives them the drugs, builds bigger prisons, passes a three-strike law and then wants us to sing "God Bless America"- no, no, no. God damn America, that's in the bible for killing innocent people, God damn America for treating our citizens as less than human. God damn America for as long as she acts like she is God and She is supreme.*"

Let me tell you, it matters where you go to church!! It matters what kind of leadership and teaching you subject yourself to, a cross on the door or a religious name is not enough, particularly these days.

Some degree in theology can be meaningless, even harmful, in the wrong hands. God's people aren't always perfect, that's why God expects us to know the Bible for ourselves. Was Obama taught to hate America for 20 years? How about scripture- 20 years of scripture learning should teach you something? Why is it missing from Obama's National Day of Prayer proclamations?

Do you think Obama refers to the Bible for wisdom and direction for one of the most powerful job on the planet? I certainly hope Obama is truly saved but here we go again, "liberal" values have quietly crept into the church, this is nothing new, it's as old as church itself. You could be in a godless liberal church today. Point is, you may just be wasting your time. The worst kind of hypocrite is a religious one- God help us all.

One of the most important decisions you can make could be "where" you attend church. I can usually spot a good church or a "dead" church within minutes. If you are unsure, pray, pray, pray. Do not stop searching until you find one.

Twenty years should easily get you a healthy knowledge of the Bible, including right living with Godly principles, and by the way a "dead" church is completely Biblical. Revelation, chapter 3, verse 1 (NAS): **"To the Angel of the Church is Sardis. I know your deeds, that you have a name that you are alive, but you are DEAD."** The chapter continues in verse 2: **"I have not found their works perfect before God,"** and Verse 3: **"repent."** So, God calls out the "dead" churches commanding them to "repent."

1 Thessalonians 4:16: "...and with the trump of God..."

Donald J. Trump
45th President 2017- PRESENT

Well known American Businessman came on the scene with no political background and won the Republican Nomination among the record-breaking number of 17 total party candidates. Trump, considered the underdog by the media, went on to defeat Hillary Clinton winning the electoral vote. Trump's popularity among his loyal constituents was fueled by his patriotism and common-sense solutions to the nation's many ills.

Trump immediately got to work fulfilling his campaign promises to the American people. Regardless of the liberal backlash, media attacks, and zero cooperation platform adopted by the Democrats, Trump's efforts to put "America First" turned the business world upside down.

His quick thinking and practical solutions began to show as corporations canceled plans to move abroad for cheap labor, which were taking America's jobs with them. Instead, one after another, companies made new commitments announcing plans to build new factories, restore our manufacturing base, while encouraging "Made in the U.S.A."

More than anything, there was a renewed hope and optimism sweeping the country and the liberals hated every minute of it. Finally, after the last eight years, the economy got a much needed "shot in the arm."

Trump didn't stop there, he ordered reviews of all U.S. Trade Agreements and went forth reversing unfair trade violations and abuses, adding to the economy. Trump took on China, which no previous President was willing or able to do, he has made progress on our border wall with Mexico, in spite of Democrats' inability to understand the concept or function of a physical barrier, except as needed for their own homes.

Trump has done everything in his power to strengthen, protect, and defend the constitution, free speech, and our religious liberties (which were slowly eroding under Obama.)

Trump passed Executive Order #13798 on May 4, 2017, "PROMOTING FREE SPEECH AND RELIGIOUS LIBERTY." Easing IRS enforcement against religious organizations who openly speak about "political issues" from a religious perspective- needed more "now" than ever. On July 3, 2020 Trump showed leadership in the wake of civil disobedience and lawlessness by signing Executive Order #13934 "BUILDING AND REBUILDING MONUMENTS TO AMERICAN HEROS." -*"These statues are not ours alone, to be discarded at the whim of those inflamed by fashionable political passions. They belong to generations that have come before us and to generations yet unborn."* Again, it is a radical, liberal, and global government eradication of our National Heroes and Monuments that help to undermine a societies' pride in their own individual unique history and heritage. Again, Trump made the right call.

The Tecumseh Curse

Ronald Reagan's failed assassination attempt seemed to break the 20 year Presidential curse. No doubt, through personal and private prayers to national prayers of Christians throughout the country, the curse was finally broken. The curse claimed seven previous Presidents, all dying while still in office, including the only four "successful" assassinations of Presidents in our history, all elected or re-elected on a "20 year" election. They include:

William Henry Harrison-Elected in 1840
Abraham Lincoln-Elected in 1860
James Garfield- Elected in 1880
William McKinley- Elected in 1900
Warren Harding-Elected in 1920
Franklin Roosevelt-Elected in 1940
John F. Kennedy-Elected in 1960

Reagan, elected in 1980, was next in line. Most people do not know what to believe when it comes to unexplained supernatural events, but curses are all too real. The Bible speaks about "generational" and other curses. They can and do exist and again are completely Biblical.

Based on my understanding of the Bible, a curse can only be broken by the power of God and in the Name of Jesus Christ. There are some curses in effect until God himself removes them, such as the curses mentioned in Genesis, at the "fall of man." However, that's not the case with the "Tecumseh" curse. This curse began when William H. Harrison who died after only one month in office, all prior Presidents were unaffected.

General Harrison, prior to his Presidency, commanded troops in the Battle of TippeCanoe (present day La Fayette, Indiana.)

The Indians, tired of broken promises, losing more territory and white expansion in the West; they desperately hoped to mount a defense and in 1811 war broke out. While the famous Shawnee Chief Tecumseh had not yet returned from his journey of trying to convince other tribal leaders to join in with their Confederacy.

Chief Tecumseh's younger brother, Tenskwatawa (known as the "prophet") attempted an early hour raid. He had hoped to gain the advantage and catch Harrison's troops off guard. Both sides suffered heavy casualties and Tenskwatawa was shamed among his people because his incantations and promises of divine protection from the enemies' musket balls had no power or effect.

Ultimately, they had to abandon their village "Prophetstown" which was burnt to the ground. The battle almost ended all hopes for an Indian Confederacy against the Western settlers. As for General Harrison, the war of 1812 was not over. In a later battle in the Battle of Thames on Oct 5, 1813, Chief Tecumseh had regrettably made an alliance with the British Army. In a last-ditch effort to turn the tide of the war, Tecumseh was ultimately killed and finally all hope was lost.

This is when, it is believed, Tenskwatawa, the prophet and Chief Tecumseh's brother, placed a curse on Harrison and the lineage of the American Presidents. The "Death of Tecumseh" (1878 immortalized painting) is viewable in the Rotunda of the U.S. Capital Building.

Because witchcraft, divination, and sorcery are strictly forbidden in scripture. This "Prophet" may have been more appropriately called a shaman or perhaps a medicine man, seer, or spiritual leader and more in line with Native American beliefs and not the Biblical definition of "prophets."

As I said, curses are Biblical, in Genesis 4 we see the first recorded curse for hands that shed innocent blood. Verse 8: **"And**

Cain talked with Abel his brother: and it came to pass, when they were in the field, that Cain rose up against Abel his brother, and slew him." verse 9: "And the LORD said unto Cain, where *is* Abel thy brother? And he said, I know not: *Am* I my brother's keeper?"

Perhaps Cain had buried the body of his brother and vainly attempted to hide his evil deeds from God. Verse 10: "**And he said, what hast thou done? The voice of thy brother's blood crieth unto me from the ground.**" Verse 11: "**And now *art* thou cursed from the earth, which hath opened her mouth to receive thy brother's blood from thy hand.**" Cain realized his punishment, and in verse 14: "**He said unto the LORD, my punishment *is* greater than I can bear. Behold, thou hast driven me out this day from the face of the Earth; and from thy face shall I be hid; and I shall be a fugitive and a vagabond in the earth; and it shall come to pass, *that* every one that findeth me shall slay me.**"

Do you recall four of the seven Presidents under the curse were assassinated or "slain" as well as Reagan's failed assassin's bullet just missing the heart? Could the "President's Curse" have been demonically empowered by the shedding of innocent blood? Only God knows for sure.

Another story in the Book of Numbers (chapter 22-24) describes a King named Balak who offered money to the Prophet Balaam if he would curse his enemies. Verse 22:6: "**Come now therefore, I pray thee, curse me this people; for they *are* too mighty for me: peradventure I shall prevail, *that* we may smite them, and *that* I may drive them out of the land: for I wot that he whom thou blessest *is* blessed, and he whom thou cursest is cursed.**" Looking at this scripture, the King knew the prophet Balaam had a powerful reputation. The King was persistent, and Balaam seemed somewhat obliged to work for the King, yet

Balaam knew he had no power to curse God's people over whom He had blessed.

After consulting with God, Balaam explained to the King in Numbers 23:20: **"Behold, I have received *commandment* to bless; and he hath blessed; and I cannot reverse it."** The Lord later said in Deuteronomy 23:5: **"Nevertheless, the LORD thy God would not hearken unto Balaam; but the Lord thy God turned the curse into a blessing unto thee, because the Lord thy God loved thee."**

There's much more written on the subject. The word "curse" or "cursed" is used 160 times in the King James Bible. If you suspect you or your family may be under a curse, it's time to call on God. There is much good Christian teaching on the subject. With the increasing popularity of witchcraft and sorcery in our culture these days, we should not be either ignorant or vulnerable on the subject.

Acts 4:26, "The kings of the earth stood up, and the rulers were gathered together against the LORD, and against his Christ."

9
World Government

s World Government imminent? Although it's hard to say for sure, just how close we are to such a radical, earthshaking change especially for us in the United States. I have made some noteworthy "observations." First, many of our older WWII generations grew up with God in their lives and still have some deeply engrained religious roots. It would be difficult for them to accept any kind of world government.

Yet, our younger generations, even particularly today's "school age" generations, have had to endure more brainwashing in terms of education and cultural decay. They are being bombarded with propaganda from the entertainment industry, including commercials, movies, cartoons, and access to the internet. They have been targeting our youth more today than at any previous time in our history. That just causes me to think that the powers that be should hope for a greater successful outcome "if they were to lay in wait" on this generation of newcomers to "come of age." Surly they have gone to extreme measures to corrupt their thinking.

That is all the more reason for us to intervene in their lives and bring them some light and truth, instead!

The Bible talks of a time in Matthew 10:21 (NLT): when, "**A brother will betray his brother to death, a father will betray his own child, and children will rebel against their parents and cause them to be killed.**" This describes to me a great disparage that will occur between generational thoughts, beliefs, ideas, and morality.

Demonically controlled liberals or the "vile" will one day turn against those of their own "household." Perhaps over "climate change hysteria" or some other fabricated World Government "greater or higher ideals" for the common man.

There will be some "perceived" need important enough, that they would be compelled to betray even their own family members.

Another clue would be the rate and degree of technological advances and breakthroughs. Though we have entered the realm of "profound" technological breakthroughs I just get the gut feeling we have a little farther to go before we can actually realize scriptural fulfillment of some scripture verses, such as the mark of the beast (Revelation 14:9) which to me this verse might describe the use of technologies, still more on the horizon, than in actual literal fulfillment today. I do not think we are far away. Time will tell! I know that many technologies already exist and are in place, yet I feel as though there is more that needs to be done! This is just my "observation" which I will not go into detail here.

Another observation about coming world government, that I will touch on, would be the danger of "fraudulent elections" in this country. Already, liberals are attempting to fundamentally change the way we vote in this nation. They are using the Covid-19 pandemic as their reason or excuse to initiate mail in voting on a large scale, while Trump rallies support for universal voter IDs.

Picture IDs of course would be difficult to fake- which are common sense, responsible safeguards, to preserve the integrity of our electoral process. We have all heard the stories of dead people voting, individuals voting multiple times, and other illegal voting scams. To liberals, stealing an election does not contradict their moral values. Lies, fraud, and thievery are just politics as usual. Again, they are willing to sacrifice the will of the people to the "higher good" of their elite aspirations. Just another "must have" effective tool for the unpopular global elites' book of tricks.

Finally, we have mentioned the "brain-washing" of our youth, fraudulent elections, and my third observation would be to cover "mass surveillance." The term "surveillance" in the Google Dictionary is defined as *"close observation, especially of a suspected spy or criminal."* When it comes to "world government" to liberals, everyone is a "suspected spy or criminal." Instead of being "innocent until proven guilty" rather you are "guilty" and the apparent "need" to monitor and compile information on your activities and behavior in their eyes is warranted.

In the old days, undercover spies had to covertly gain access to a target's house, place of work, or meeting place. Then they would have to physically plant a hidden "bug" or listening device. Whereas today, people literally buy similar 'listening devices" and unwittingly "plant" them in their homes themselves, all in the name of convenience. I am talking about "voice assistants" such as "Siri" or "Alexa" and similar artificial intelligence technology that respond to your voice commands, obviously these devices are equipped with high quality microphones, and can capture your voice within close proximity to the device. How difficult would it be to remotely enable the device to eavesdrop on your conversations? Let me say, you would really have to be a trusting person to not think that these devices might be used against you one day in the future.

Most of us have been aware for decades now that our common everyday technologies contain the ability to invade are privacy, yet I do not think that most of us are aware of just how "broad in scope" these capabilities exist . This is particularly true as is the case today with our "hard to live without" cell phones, and daily internet usage.

Many of these devices have the potential to eavesdrop on our conversations. Today, the powers that be monitor our conversations. Save and store text messages and e-mails, monitor our patterns of behavior, and track our everyday movements.

Whether through modern technology or the "old fashioned" way, paranoid governments and tyrants have always found new and inventive techniques to monitor the behaviors of their people. So, I think there has been a "shift" taking place. There has been an apparent need and desire for our government and others to compile (once considered private) information on every individual.

These "needs" evidently, far exceed their citizens' right to privacy. These "privacy rights" violations should have no part in a free society, except for certain circumstances which would require adhering to strict protocols based on probable cause. Requiring a specific warrant and signed by a Judge. That was the law of the land in the days prior to the 9/11 terrorist attacks.

With safeguards in place, this should remain the law of the land. Unfortunately, this is simply not the case in todays' America. This is a broad topic, there is more to cover on this subject. However, for now, this is yet another sign or precursor to the prevailing intrusion into the daily lives of good and honest law-abiding citizens. These are common tactics amongst tyrannical, oppressive, and controlling governments. China for one, would be a great example of a government "drunk" and obsessed with "mass surveillance."

That being said- what are the "signs" of coming world government to our Hometown U.S.A.? The idea of world government is nothing new. People have written about it and speculated about it from our ancient roots to our recent past. Therefore, there is no shortage of information on the subject.

Men have debated and devised methods they deem vital and worthy to bring about their desired World Government. Though I am using caution when it comes to predicting or date-setting. Yet, when I look for the "signs" (right here in America, right here and now) I can say without reservation that I am shocked at what I see.

Though we could have years and years to prepare ourselves, things could literally happen almost "overnight." Perhaps the single greatest issue now, in our American culture, would be the widespread liberal-controlled mass media or "fake-news" bought and paid for by enemies of religious conservatives.

These include unjust censorship of nearly every popular social media platform. (and they have deep pockets). They consider our disagreement with their liberal-social ideals as nothing more than "hate speech." Christian moral standards are labeled hateful and therefore can be removed, manipulated, and defunded. Ultimately, they want to censor or silence free speech in this country. These actions would help them to insure the free flow of their ungodly values and ideals. I thank God, that even, "in spite" of their worse efforts, they have not completely silenced conservative thought or speech.

Thankfully, many of our liberal "great media institutions" today suffer from historically "poor ratings." This is good news, as it helps to undermine their ability to continue to defraud the American public.

It is tragic for Americans and Trump haters that they can't see or realize God's hand on the affairs of American politics and culture. Yet to overcome America's great "thorn in the side" of global-elites, they must attempt to control thought via liberal mass-media propaganda. Of course, it's not difficult to see the fruit of decade long efforts and planning via liberal global activists.

It is almost as if America has been this great "up and coming" train wreck. We have been heading down the tracks of no return, to certain disaster, resulting from all the enemies' energy and efforts over the past decades. Yet, all a sudden, God steps in and intervenes and says no! And God says- "I have not forgotten AMERICA"!

Here is a "semi-famous" quote from James Warburg on Feb 17, 1950 while he spoke to the U.S. Senate Committee on foreign relations. *"We shall have world government, whether or not we like it. The question is only whether world government will be achieved by consent or conquest."*

I know that presently America will not accept world government by consent. With God's favor on our side and Trump at the helm of another 4 years, I see it highly unlikely that America could allow such a dramatic change. Although, some "Earth shattering" event could turn that on a dime. That may be the catalyst indeed needed to produce such a radical turnaround.

Well, while in the midst of a worldwide event with the Covid-19 pandemic right now, I don't believe this is the "Earth shattering" event that I'm referring to, but what about a "nuclear" sized event? Even on our shores within the homeland of America- is that a possible future scenario? Some "State of Emergency" could bring America to the brink of dramatic and fundamental change.

Liberals find it difficult to show any "real leadership" in time of crisis, rather, they would easily follow the whim of any "global" united opinion on the matter. They would quickly "jump onboard" with any so-called viable plan or solution provided them, even a United Nation's third world solution would sound good to them. That is certainly one scenario.

I hope America can be United once again, "One Nation Under God" sure sounds beautiful! Somehow, I get this nagging feeling that for the most part, the liberals are not going away. They may go into hiding, as they may be defeated at the polls, but I think the "liberals will do liberal things."- Isaiah 32:8 says: **"But the liberal deviseth liberal things; and by liberal things shall he stand."**

I pray that great number of liberals will come to the genuine saving knowledge of Jesus Christ, turn from their wicked ways, and be converted. Just as I did. That would be great!! I just think they'll be some waiting, watching, and "lying in wait" ready to exploit the right opportunity and the "right conditions" and the right maybe "catastrophe" to sell out America.

If they ever get their "claws" and their "teeth" fully into the reign of power again, with the right conditions, I believe it would be disastrous for America. At that point, our only hope will be to wait it out until the much anticipated, "return of Christ."

Even our own history should teach us about Nazi-Germany and their insatiable need or desire to rely so heavily on the "feeding" of a public with a constant diet of calculated, deliberate, deceptive mass media propaganda. So too would any "world government" who must deceive the masses, for the purpose of controlling them. That is what it all boils down to, yes, it is all about "control."

Only through mass-propaganda, can they realize their evil ambitions. That is, without the interference of good and righteous people. To unite their cause and to silence detractors, a constant diet of "state-run" premeditated mass media must occur, it is vital to perpetuating their lies and deception.

The scriptures speak about a **"time of wars and rumors of wars"**- Matthew 24:6: Dictionary.com defines a rumor as: *"a story or statement in general circulation without confirmation or certainty as to the facts."* I believe this verse parallels a time in our history during World War II. Hitler and the Nazi's were filling their "concentration camps" with unsuspected victims. These poor souls were boarded on train cars and given specific instructions on the amount of luggage they would be permitted to carry, to some newly relocated destination. Of course, tragically, this was a complete deception.

Their "final destination" was Hitler's "final solution." Suddenly, their thoughtfully prepared luggage meant nothing while their very lives and the lives of their loved ones were in immediate peril.

I have read of actual accounts in which *"rumors"* were spread among passengers of the "real intent" for their pondered train ride, however, with no real proof or real evidence, many decent people simply decided to just trust and hope for the best. It has been speculated that even the allies were not aware of Hitler's "final solution" until after they liberated the actual concentration camps to see for themselves.

What would have happened if they had known the truth? Well, maybe they could have spent the time saying goodbye, praying, and encouraging and strengthening their loved ones. Perhaps, some may have escaped, even getting the word out to allied governments. Perhaps, "united" they could have even mounted a defense. Instead, they were like "sheep led to the slaughter." You know, "Good News" can go a long way to strengthen a man's heart. Unfortunately, the tyrants know this as well.

There are "state-controlled media institutions" that are fully in existence today. Just look at China, North Korea, don't forget Saddam controlled Iraq, for a short-list. These are a few examples where every word goes through a propaganda filter, first and foremost, formulated to bring some desired result. Truth is "absolutely meaningless" to these Dictators. To them, only holding on to "reigns" of power, at the expense of the people, is a means to an end.

Have we arrived there yet? Of course not. However, can you simply see how much easier it would be for them? A large majority of mindless liberal media institutions are already up and running, and watched daily in America? All you need to do is fax or email them the latest world government "talking points" or other news- worthy or unworthy updates, lies and manipulations.

I couldn't tell you how many people still trust the liberal "Anti-Trump" news media. I tell everyone I know to make the switch to historically accurate, truthful, trustworthy conservative based media. Some people just do not understand that they are being manipulated; they blindly trust these news agencies. They are unaware of any change in their character or operations.

Is it already too late for some people, or do we continue to hold out hope? Only God knows for sure. If I go out, I want to "go out fighting" for the truth!

George Washington once said, "*If Freedom of Speech is taken away, then dumb and silent we may be led like sheep to the slaughter.*" The truth should always be worth fighting for. I don't want to be a "lamb or sheep led to the slaughter," nor do I want anyone, especially family and friends. I want to be the lamb that looks the wolf in the eyes while he's second guessing his next move. Amen.

Even so, LORD JESUS COME!!!!

10

Conclusion

The precious freedoms we enjoy in this country, the envy of the world, may easily be taken for granted. They are every bit worth fighting for, they may in fact require our due diligence by all those who now stand for these truths. I believe we are called at this time to make that stand, fearless of the intimidation and propaganda so prevalent in todays' society.

We are called to know the truth. We should not fail to be counted among the righteous, by casting our ballot (a statement of faith for the principles and moral values held dearly by our Founding Fathers.) That means not succumbing to the temptation to remain "silent" in this crucial hour.

Not voting, staying home on election day, or failure to act, could be considered a cowardly act or a lack of concern for our young ones, future generations, and our children and grandchildren in this country. We must "stand in the gap" for them. Our younger generation desperately need men and women as role models, guides who will make a stand for truth and righteousness, regardless of cost.

You know, "One Nation under God" requires all parties to be submitted unto God. That is hardly the reality today. The good people of this country are not giving up easily. We will not give up without a fight.

They say in the song, The Star-Spangled Banner, that America is the "land of the free, and the home of the brave." This is our legacy. You know from time to time and throughout history, men and women are required to stand against tyranny and wickedness with ungodliness, this is one of those times in this country.

Are you awake?! Can you see what's going on? Do you perceive the threat coming against our country?! Will you stand for freedom? Will we have another chance to stand for the truth in honest and free elections in this country? That's a good question. Hopefully, we will, yet it may be wise to prepare for the worst! Time will tell.

If Trump did not win in 2016 election, we may have already found ourselves succumbed to some liberal, progressive, United Nations mandated ill willed agenda and relinquishing of our sovereign rights to self-govern. Believe me! You do not want to live under a liberal world government society.

Today, America is still the best example throughout the world of a good and proper government, which is upheld by Almighty God and a just, moral, and upright people. America is a light to oppressed people throughout the world. People do not try and immigrate to communist, socialist, or dictatorial nations. Many times, people desperately try and escape those countries and their oppressive regimes.

The Bible teaches that there is coming a world government under the leadership of Jesus Christ. This "time period" is referred to in scripture as the one thousand year, or "millennial" reign of Christ. This will be a fantastic time to be alive! Revelations 20:4: **"and they lived and reigned with Christ a thousand years."** However, prior to that event, the antichrist will attempt to bring the entire world under Satan's control. The Bible predicts this and yes it will happen as it is written!

Interestingly, Adolph Hitler (an early manifestation of the antichrist) boasted of a "thousand-year reich" or a thousand-year reign of Nazi-rule. Thank God he was unable to perform it. Yet, it appears he was trying to prevent Christ's second coming by fulfilling the scripture himself. Let me tell you, I would certainly prefer to see our nation not bow its knee to the antichrist, or at least not without a fight.

Fight the good fight of faith: 1 Timothy 6:12: **"Fight the good fight of faith, lay hold on eternal life, to which you were also called."** Teach your children truth! Memorize scripture, practice prayer, get healthy, have extra emergency supplies, food, medicine, etc., on hand. Think about worse case scenarios. Find ways to secure and defend yourselves and family in case of emergency. Consider possible scenarios such as social unrest, upheaval and lawlessness, natural and man-made disasters, wartime, hostile foreign governments, terrorist attacks or pandemics, etc.

Proverbs 22:3 (NLT), says, **"A prudent person foresees danger and takes precautions. The simpleton goes blindly on and suffers the consequences."**

This verse needs no explanation, Also, Proverbs 10:5: **"He that gathereth in summer is a wise son: but he that sleepeth in harvest is a son that causes shame."** The Bible says to consider the ant. Proverbs 6:6-8 (MSG) Version: **"Look at the ant, watch it closely, let it teach you a thing or two. Nobody has to tell it what to do. All summer it stores up food; at harvest it stockpiles provisions."**

Prepare! Prepare! Prepare! It's the "new reality." It is certainly easier to do in a good economy, and I believe without a doubt that a Trump win in 2020 will be our best chance for a good, if not great, economy again. Perhaps only for a limited time! Perhaps only for a season. By the election of Donald Trump in 2020, we would at least be "buying ourselves precious time" for ourselves and our families. I believe God is wanting to give us "more grace." I don't know about you, but I will take all the grace I can get.

Liberals are not afraid of destroying our economy. I guess they believe a dead U.S.A. would be good for the planet. They would prefer to see America become a heap of ashes then to give up their power-hungry ways! Many of these ungodly politicians use the power and influence of their political office to personally enrich themselves and their family members.

1 Samuel 8:3 (NIRV) says, **"...they were only interested in making money. They accepted money from people who wanted special favors. They made things that were wrong, appear to be right."** I tell you this great United States has been their personal bank account for so long, they cannot even think of leading a good and honest life. Some boast of huge net-worth and hefty bank accounts, far beyond their actual salaries. In some cases, these are the results of under-handed deals, and politically and financially motivated favors. All the while fueling anti-American, immoral, and unjust behavior. Even at the cost of treason to the average American taxpayer.

These corrupt politicians travel by private jet, stay at luxury hotels, including extravagant meals and limousines, all to their "save the planet" conferences. In truth, they are hypocritical, and I for one refuse to accept their propaganda. They oftentimes cater to large corporations, guilty more so themselves for their unre-strained and environmentally irresponsible profit driven motives. Again, the ungodly! They desire to blame and oppress the people while they ignore the rules themselves.

I choose to let God, the creator of all, create a new planet, on His own time frame, according to His infinite wisdom, and according to His plan and purpose for mankind. In the meantime, I will try to be a conscientious and good steward of His resources.

Worshiping the "creator more than his creation." Romans 1:25, says, **"They exchanged the truth of God for a lie, and worshiped and served created things rather than the Creator, who is forever worthy of praise!" Amen!**

Let me say first and foremost, God's priority is your relationship with Him that you are in right standing with Him! Then, when you begin to study the scriptures and read the Bible for yourself, you will no doubt become a believer and supporter of "Christian conservative values and a purveyor of good moral judgement." Armed with that knowledge, you will become highly qualified to cast your ballot responsibly in any fair election.

However, if you vote based on criteria such as personality, hair color, or gentlemen like qualities, or lack thereof, then God help us. Because this type of anti-Trump hatred and excuses for not voting Trump, even though he is scripturally correct (not politically, so called correct) will spell disaster for this country. It was Thomas Jefferson that said, "On matters of style, swim with the current, on matters of principle, stand like a rock." These are certainly great words of wisdom that apply to our day!

It seems that some people have simply lost their moral compass! Sadly, there are still way too many people who give their blind allegiance to and cast their ballot for the next "up and coming liberal charismatic leader." Yes, I am talking about the "antichrist." Daniel 11:21 says, **"...there shall stand up a vile person."** Surely there will be those who will receive him with open arms! I do not think he will be a conservative! No, I am quite sure he will be a liberal!

Trump, of course, is not a perfect man. No one is, God is not looking for perfect people, he is looking for willing people! I sincerely believe God has prepared Trump for this hour, maybe all his life, long before any of us knew he was even interested in politics. His sometimes "rash" or rude behavior, name calling, and insults or whatever character attacks he's been accused of, are all (what I believe) are "fair game" when you consider the "character of the enemy" that he or should I say "we" are up against.

Does anyone remember a time in this country when journalists upheld a high standard of ethics? They would strive to be fair, unbiased and honest. They took personal responsibility for reporting the most accurate truthful and up to date information available. They were reliable and trustworthy.

However, todays', liberal "journalists" have resorted to an all-out war with Trump, fueled by their extreme hatred of this President. It appears that ethical behavior no longer applies to them. With a never-ending barrage of accusations and fault finding against this "fairly elected President." It is only their destruction of Donald Trump and the smell of his blood that alone satisfies their appetites.

So, you know, average "gentleman," that is a "gentle" man, would have clearly gave up the fight by now. God needed a man with some "grit," maybe a little resolve, tough as nails, a fighter, a man that could go twelve rounds. Anything less, he would become a statistic of the liberal left who has deep pockets and an even deeper, or should I say "darker," rule book.

The tactics and ploys of the sinister, and I mean sinister globalist elites, hold no bounds. Every form of decency, fair play, and rule of law is out the window. They seek to destroy Trump and could care less about the will of the people expressed through free and fair elections. They no longer honor the outcome of our electoral process.

Trump is on the front lines of the fight to protect and uphold the Constitution of the United States. Too many people still don't even realize our nation's sovereign existence is in danger. If you're fighting an alley cat, let me tell you, you don't appeal to their "higher good." No, you get down in the trenches and give them all you've got. That alley cat's not going to respect you until you swing him around by his tail for a bit!! And that's being kind!

The voice of the propaganda machine was caught off guard when Trump began his campaign to the American people on Twitter. They could have not possibly perceived Trump's uncanny ability to either bypass them completely or to fight back constantly and consistently. He also regularly reminds the people to not blindly trust in our once beloved iconic news media institutions. For they no longer speak the truth.

These days you "gotta be a brawler" to survive the front lines, surely Trump is on the front lines. He's taken a lot of hits for the American people. He most certainly is standing in the gap for the average Christian in this country. As Christians, we need to consistently pray and stand in the gap for him and his family, and don't forget fellow conservatives by his side.

How short is the memory of some, I remember a time only a few short years ago when the prevailing thought was to silence the truth in this country Christian ideals were not considered free speech. Pastors were being threatened with jail time for speaking out against homosexuality as written in scripture. A time where good and just morals came under attack.

Christian businesses could no longer exercise their freedom to practice their good conscience. Pastors were informed they needed to provide copies of their sermons for scrutiny by local governments, the "hate speech police."

Are we just one Presidential election away from tyranny? It is time to fight for the soul of this country. Without a good moral backbone, we are doomed. The enemy wants to erase our Christian heritage and I for one, want to fight to preserve it. This is what made America great.

What will it take to get you off the couch in November? I believe God is on our side and just hope that the prevailing wind is in our favor, yet good people must make a stand. The threat has not gone away, it is just waiting for another opportunity to rear its ugly head.

Together, let's not give them that opportunity! Let's stand and be counted. Let's teach our sons and daughters to stand for the greater good. Let's teach them about our Godly heritage. Don't allow Hollywood and the pervasive culture dictate to our precious children's receptive, yet vulnerable minds. Put down the remote control and control our own outcomes, for a change!

We can help future generations with their knowledge and understanding of the truth. Let's put some good controls in place. Let's put some good habits into practice. One generation could change the course of this world and the enemy is all too aware of this. If we understand his tactics, we can undermine his efforts.

Please, put down your cell phones for a minute, and spend some "vital" time on our knees, for our families, and for our country's sake. We've got to change our habits. We are in a battle, and most of us are asleep, or preoccupied with worldly pursuits. Can we sacrifice a few more days of living in our "make believe" worlds and get serious about the future?

We must educate ourselves. Seek out timeless truths within the pages of the Bible. Find a good Bible believing church, get involved, and help support them financially. Be an example for your family. Attend church regularly. Spend money on Christian resources and make time for GOD in your life. And do not take todays' freedoms for granted.

Many soldiers have shed their blood to ensure your freedoms Now those freedoms are in jeopardy once more. These times call for a reaction from you. Don't sit idly by hoping someone else will carry your cross. We ALL must do our part, only then are we strong! "Land of the free, home of the brave" they say! I pray they were right!!!

Photo/Image Credits

1 (Tower of Babel) Artist: lian_2011/Shutterstock.com

2 (Bibles) Artist: Lincoln Rogers/Shutterstock.com

3 (Liberal) Artist: Contimis Works/Shutterstock.com

4 (King David) Artist: Only Fabrizio/Shutterstock.com-sculpture by Adamo Tadolini

5 (Polling place) Artist: Rob Crandall/Shutterstock.com

6 (Rip) Photo by MANDEL NGAN/AFP via Getty Images

7 (Clap) Photo by Doug Mills-Pool/Getty Images

8 (General Assembly) Artist: Drop of Light/Shutterstock.com

9 (Secretary Generals) Artist: Tookrub/shutterstock.com

10 (King Solomon) Artist: Morphart Creation/Shutterstock.com

11 (Human fetus/12 weeks) Artist: Steve Allen/Shutterstock.com

12 (Border Wall) Artist: Sherry V Smith/Shutterstock.com

13 (WTC 9/11) Artist: Photo by CNN via Getty Images

14 (Crowd) Artist: Anton Gvozdikov/Shetterstock.com

15 (Journalist) Artist: Sharomka/Shutterstock.com

16 (Boots) Artist: David Tran/Shutterstock.com

17 (Rainbow Flag) Artist: Marc Bruxelle/Shutterstock.com

18 (Gun) Artist: thipjang/Shutterstock.com— sculpture by Fredrik Reutersward at United Nations Headquarters

19 (Pollution) Artist: Vadim Petrakov/Shutterstock.com

20 (Military) Artist: Meysam Azarneshin/ Shutterstock.com

21 (Trump Tower) Artist: Jarrod Ryan Jooste/Shutterstock.com

22 (Washington) Artist: Everett Collection/ Shutterstock.com-oil on canvas by Gilbert Stuart

23 (Lincoln) Artist: Everett Collection/ Shutterstock.com

24 (Reagan) Artist: Mark Reinstein/ Shutterstock.com

25 (Obama) Artist: Everett Collection/ Shutterstock.com

26 (Trump) Artist: Grindstone Media Group/Shutterstock.com

27 (Dollar) Artist: Nosyrevy/Shutterstock.com

CPSIA information can be obtained
at www.ICGtesting.com
Printed in the USA
LVHW010342111220
673819LV00039B/2503